CAESAR
AS MAN OF LETTERS

CAESAR

AS MAN OF
LETTERS

BY

F. E. ADCOCK

ARCHON BOOKS
1969

FIRST PUBLISHED 1956
BY THE SYNDICS OF THE CAMBRIDGE UNIVERSITY PRESS
REPRINTED 1969 WITH PERMISSION
OF THE CAMBRIDGE UNIVERSITY PRESS
IN AN UNALTERED AND UNABRIDGED EDITION

SBN: 208 00727 X
LIBRARY OF CONGRESS CATALOG CARD NUMBER: 69-13622
PRINTED IN THE UNITED STATES OF AMERICA

CONTENTS

v

PREFACE

THE purpose of this book is to emphasize the literary character of the writings of Caesar that have survived. The use of these works as an introduction to the translation of Latin is justified by the high degree of lucidity which they possess, and the comparatively limited vocabulary which they employ. But when they have served this practical purpose in schools, Caesar's writings tend to be neglected. The early introduction often does not lead to a further, more interested, acquaintanceship. There is a temptation to believe that the perusal of one or two of the *Commentaries* provides so fair a sample of them all that that is enough. And the appetite for reading Caesar's works for pleasure may have been dulled by the recollection of the effort once needed to read them at all. Finally, it is easy to believe that what was intelligible to the Fourth Form is not worthy of the attention of the Sixth, much less of the attention of undergraduates.

When I was reading for the Classical Tripos I was not urged to peruse any part of Caesar's *Commentaries*: I could be trusted to be generally aware of their contents from history books, and there were other more varied, more mellifluous, models of Latin prose style to assist my efforts at composition. And, unless my memory betrays me, no scholar in the University of Cambridge has, in the last half century, devoted even the shortest of lecture courses to the works of Caesar. There are, no doubt, other authors with a better claim on the attention of lecturers, either because of their greater literary appeal or because of their greater difficulty, or because they illuminate more clearly a phase of Latin literature or Roman thought. But, none the less, it is worth while to read Caesar; and, if he is read, he may be read with more interest and understanding if the reader can turn to some book or other which may assist him to appreciate, so far as the efforts of scholars have been fruitful, the literary character of Caesar's writings and the way in which they reflect his eminent personality.

In pursuit of this practical purpose it is convenient to begin with a brief Introduction to remind the reader of what Caesar was when his works were in the making. A complete account of his career and historical significance would pass beyond the scope of this particular study. This Introduction is followed by a discussion of the literary form to which the *Commentaries* belong, even though, as will be seen, they have qualities which are not narrowly limited by the convention of the form. Caesar was not concerned merely to follow a model or to be guided by a convention, but in so far as he did follow it, it is desirable to have an idea what the model was. Then follows a chapter on the purpose and content of the *Commentaries*, which may assist the reader to judge the effect of the convention on what Caesar wrote and the degree to which he goes beyond it. The recurrent theme of the *Commentaries* is war, and in the next chapter 'The "Military Man"' Caesar's literary interpretation of war and of its protagonists is described. This leads on to the consideration of style as the revelation of Caesar's personality as well as his way of writing.

These chapters, taken together, form the main stock of the book for most of the readers for whom it is intended. But there are certain questions which have been warmly debated by many scholars for many years. It is hard to study Caesar's writings intensively for quite a long time without trying to be as sure as one can be about these matters, and the chapter entitled 'Certain Problems' is intended to offer arguments in support of some conclusions which appear the most probable. Finally, there is a short characterization of other works which belong to the Corpus of *Commentaries* on Caesar's campaigns and may be compared and contrasted with his own writings.

The activity of scholars during the last hundred years or so has produced a very large literature on Caesar's writing. I have tried to take account of most of this literature and am, needless to say, much indebted to it, but I have limited my references to it to the acknowledgements of some particular obligation or so as to suggest to a reader some work of particular importance. To add a bibliography which would be, in any sense, representative of the literature would add unduly to the size of the book. The Index of Passages, which follows the General Index, may be useful to some readers. The readings in these passages normally follow the latest edition of Klotz's Teubner text.

I have to acknowledge advice and criticism of many friends, either given in conversation or after reading parts or the whole of the book at various stages in its composition. In particular, I am indebted to my friends Mr G. T. Griffith, Mr N. G. L. Hammond, Dr A. H. McDonald and Professor E. T. Salmon in this respect. For errors of fact or doctrine I remain entirely responsible.

F. E. A

CAMBRIDGE
January 1955

INTRODUCTION

WHEN Caesar set out for Gaul in March 58 B.C. (at an age when Alexander was dead and Napoleon defeated)[1] he was Pontifex Maximus and a consular, a governor of two provinces, a general with a small army which might be increased at need. He had been an adventurous politician, who had evaded or surmounted the dangers that beset the advance to high office of a man whose early connexions had been suspect, who had been a spendthrift, a fashionable gallant, not made respectable by bribing his way to the headship of the State religion. He had displayed force as an orator and dexterity in intrigue. He had achieved some military success as propraetor in Spain and repaired his fortune which had hitherto needed the support of the great financier Crassus repaid by political services. A timely adherence to Pompey, who had been alienated by the ill will of the influential aristocrats who served and were served by the convention of Senatorial government, had given him the opportunity of reconciling Crassus and Pompey in a coalition in which he was a partner, but hardly a partner on equal terms. They had procured for him election to the consulship in which

[1] G. Boissier, *Cicéron et ses amis*, p. 242.

he had served their interests and his own, while at the same time finding scope for some practical reforms in the control of provincial government. The drastic use of his position and of the forces at the disposal of the coalition had broken through conventional hindrances and he had openly exulted at the helplessness of his enemies. As proconsul of Cisalpine Gaul he was to have an army to act as the military reserve of the coalition for the next few years. Then the province of Transalpine Gaul had fallen vacant and had been added to his command, so that his ambition now had a wider scope. It would be possible for him to gather to himself a following of soldiers as his *legati*, to find a post for the son of Crassus and employment for the talents of Labienus, who was probably a *protégé* of Pompey. But when all was added together, Caesar had not, so far, achieved the eminence that is attributed to him by the biographical tradition that has anticipated his future greatness.

During the good fighting season of eight years Caesar was campaigning beyond the Alps. In most winters he was engaged in the duties of a governor in Northern Italy, duties which to a man of his power of rapid work would leave him time to write an account of his campaigns if he wished to do so.

He would be in touch with the course of political events in Rome, and when the coalition was in danger of breaking up early in 56 B.C., he was able to meet his political allies in conferences at Ravenna and Luca, and it may be assumed that his tact was efficacious in removing the jealous distrust which haunted the relations of Pompey and Crassus. His dispatches to the Senate, more voluminous, it seems, than was usual, were read in the Curia and were no doubt talked about in aristocratic circles. The thanksgivings that were voted would advertise the victories they celebrated. When Cicero delivered his speech *On the Consular Provinces* in 56 he assumed that the Senators knew roughly what Caesar had achieved. There was a lively correspondence between Caesar himself and his officers and other friends at Rome, and it is possible that men in his confidence visited Rome and were visited by Romans. Roman opinion and Caesar were thus not without contact with each other. But it is probable, though it is not certain, that Caesar did not publish his *Commentaries* year by year, even if, as seems at least likely, he wrote them year by year (see below, pp. 77 ff.). Then, probably late in 51 or early in 50, the first seven books of the *Gallic War* were published describing Caesar's *res gestae* in Gaul to the fall of Alesia, the crowning mercy which removed the last resistance that could hope to defeat outright his purposes. What followed in the two years after Alesia was left to be described by Hirtius, a member of his staff who enjoyed his confidence.

Had the Civil War not broken out, Caesar's seven *Commentaries* would justify his claim to a triumph, his election as consul and possibly the conferring on

3   1-2

him of a second great command as proconsul. As it was, they had placed on record the fact that he had deserved better of the Republic than to be denied the satisfaction of his ambition. Whatever the outcome of Caesar's invasion of Italy, his *res gestae* in Gaul had been placed above dispute. But, after a long-drawn crisis at Rome, Caesar had to resort to war to make good his claims, matching his own genius and his own army against the power of the Republic so far as this lay in the hands of his enemies. The three books of the *Civil War* reveal a Caesar who was determined to have his way. During the two years that are described, Caesar was at pains to justify himself and was prepared to seek an end to what he calls a *civilis dissensio*, provided he was placed above any danger from his enemies and any disappointment of his ambitions. It may seem to us that Caesar's greatness and the continuance of the aristocratic Republic ruled each other out, that the State was already what Caesar was to call 'a phantom without substance'. During his years in Gaul his single will had prevailed, and when he returned to Rome in 47 B.C. he was more prepared to pardon his enemies and reward his friends than to place himself on a level with the Senate and People of Rome. He was a dictator as Sulla had been, but he presently declared that Sulla had been an innocent (*litteras nescisse*) when he abdicated. It is, as will be seen, disputable when the three books of these *Commentaries* were published,

4

but it is at least very probable that they were written when Caesar was not yet determined to set a personal autocracy, or, as many suppose, a Hellenistic monarchy, in the place of the traditional Republic. He had crossed the Rubicon, but he had not crossed the watershed that divides an *imperator* of the Roman Republic from an Emperor of Rome. The *Civil War* should then be read as, above all, the work of a man fighting for his life and his career, whatever more distant visions of statesmanship may have haunted his dreams.

I

THE LITERARY FORM

THE extant continuous writings of Caesar were entitled *C. Iuli Caesaris commentarii rerum gestarum*. After the researches of F. W. Kelsey,[1] this seems to be beyond doubt, and it has not been seriously doubted. What we possess must have been contained in nine rolls—the first seven books of the *Gallic War*, covering the years 58–52 B.C. being rolls I–VII; then roll IX—the first two books of the *Civil War* covering the year 49; and roll X the third book of the *Civil War* describing the events of 48 B.C. until the narrative breaks off late in that year. Between roll VII and roll IX there lay the eighth book of the *Gallic War*, written by Hirtius, and the series of commentaries in the Caesarian Corpus was completed by the addition of three rolls containing the *Bellum Alexandrinum*, the *Bellum Africum* or *Africanum*, and *Bellum Hispaniense*. The whole series thus describes the military achievements of Caesar from the moment he arrived in Gaul in 58 B.C. to his victory over the younger Cn. Pompeius in 45 B.C. and its immediate consequences. Caesar's authorship of rolls I–VII, IX and X was no secret in his own times and it is hard to believe that

[1] 'The title of Caesar's Work', *Trans. Amer. Phil. Assoc.* XXXVI (1905), pp. 211–38.

it was ever concealed. They reveal at first hand the mind of the man whose exploits they describe, and it must have been at once plain that no one else can have written them. The theme of Caesar's commentaries is his *res gestae* whether in Gaul or in the theatres of war of that part of the *Bellum Civile*—or, as Caesar called it, the *civilis dissensio*—of which he himself wrote. By the time of Suetonius a distinction was made between Caesar's account of events in Gaul and his account of the Civil War, but, primarily, the simple description of the theme was *res gestae*.

A *commentarius* was a form of composition that already had a long history. The word corresponds in Latin to the Greek word *hypomnema*, which may be translated *aide-mémoire*, and the Greek word and its Latin equivalent are used of written matter that serves the purpose of an *aide-mémoire*. The origin of such writings is, primarily, official or private, and it is found in the times of Alexander the Great and his successors, an inheritance from the practice of Oriental monarchies so far as it was not the natural product of administrative convenience. On the military side, *hypomnemata* might be the war-diaries of generals, dispatches and reports such as have been found in a papyrus of the reign of Ptolemy VIII. In civil administration they may be memoranda or bureaucratic records. They may be Court journals in the Hellenistic kingdoms and so on. They are not, to begin with, intended for publication. In private life they may be written material for speeches—at least the word 'commentarius' is used in Cicero of the notes for a speech—or they may be private papers and memoranda. Thus Caelius[1] sends to Cicero, then governing Cilicia, a 'commentarius rerum urbanarum' which contains a catalogue of events at Rome for Cicero's information. Not all of it, Caelius implies, is worth Cicero's attention: 'ex quo tu quae digna sunt selige'. So far, it may be said that *hypomnemata* or *commentarii* are, in general, statements of facts for their own sake, so far as they are not just helps to memory; though, inevitably, they may contain the facts as they are discerned by their authors. Such are *commentarii* in their origin. Literary merit is not their concern. They should be precise and clear, or they would defeat their own purpose, and that is all.

In contrast to these there is *historia*. To the Romans, of Caesar's day and afterwards, *historia* was, above all, an achievement of literary art. It is to Quintilian 'proxima poetis et quodammodo carmen solutum'.[2] The author of a work of *historia* was, above all, a stylist: what he regarded as fine writing was his chief aim, and not the discovery of truth. This does not mean that his work should not be credible or sincere—Livy is sincere even when he cannot be judged credible—but the merit of *historia* and the merit of establishing truth of fact are not one merit but two. The 'brevitas' of Sallust, 'primus Romana Crispus in historia',[3] is

---

[1] *ad Fam.* VIII, 11, 4.   [2] *Inst. Or.* X, 1, 31.   [3] Martial, XIV, 191, 2.

8

unlike enough to the 'lactea ubertas' of Livy, but what they are both concerned with, above all, is the same thing, a literary achievement.

Between *commentarius* of the original type and *historia* there is room for something which is not quite either the one or the other, something more than the first in content and less than the second in style. It is a development of the *commentarius*, and it is, as has been well observed,[1] something more Roman than Greek. This intermediate stage had been attained before the time of Caesar. Commentaries of this kind may be the material which the writer of *historia* can take and transmute by the alchemy of his literary art. This had been realized as will be seen presently, and it finds a place in Lucian's essay *Quomodo historia scribenda est.*[2] Such a *commentarius* of the intermediate stage may have absorbed or digested *commentarii* of the original type, or worked them together into a narrative which is not yet *historia* but has attained that synoptic view of events which Polybius claimed to have achieved. It is a natural process, and it is natural that it should be applied by the person most concerned with the events it describes. But it remains a *commentarius* until the man of letters converts it into *historia*. Though the author of the *commentarius* may describe things from his own standpoint, it still purports to be a statement of the facts for their own sake.

[1] By F. Jacoby, *Die Fragm. der griech. Historiker*, II D, pp. 639 f.
[2] 48 ff.

The development of the commentary to be the material of *historia* may conveniently be illustrated from a letter written by Lucius Verus to his tutor, Fronto.[1] The letter was written in A.D. 165, but the practical and psychological processes are near enough to those of the last decades of the Republic. Verus had been the nominal architect of a victory over the Parthians, though the strategical plan had been devised by Marcus Aurelius and had been executed by two able generals, Avidius Cassius and Martius Verus. Lucius Verus, a prince in search of a panegyrist, writes to Fronto to say he is forwarding the dispatches of his subordinates and has directed the two generals to draw up *commentarii* describing their operations for Fronto's use. He then offers to prepare a *commentarius* of his own in whatever form his tutor suggests. 'I am ready', he says, 'to fall in with your suggestions, provided my exploits are put by you in a bright light. Of course you will not overlook my *orationes* to the Senate and *adlocutiones* to my army.' Thus Fronto will have material for the speeches that were an adornment of *historia*. 'My *res gestae*', Verus concludes, 'whatever their character, are of course no greater than they actually are, but they will appear to be as great as you wish them to appear to be.' Fronto did not refuse this naïve request, and there have survived some fragmentary specimens of the preamble to the *historia*, which he probably did not

[1] In *ad Verum Imp.* II, 3.

live to complete. The *commentarius* material placed at Fronto's disposal thus ranges from matter of the original type to the more advanced form. It awaits conversion into the full-dress literary form of the *historia*, which, to judge from the fragments of the preamble, would have been full-dress indeed.

What Lucius Verus had done, Cicero had done before him, if with less *naïveté*. In June 60 B.C. he wrote in Greek a *commentarius consulatus sui* and sent it to Poseidonius, the leading Greek man of letters of the day, with the request that he would treat of these events '*ornatius*'. Poseidonius neatly replied that when he read the *commentarius* he did not feel bold enough to attempt the theme.[1] Four years later Cicero tried again. He encouraged the Roman man of letters, L. Lucceius, to write a *historia* which would include the Catilinarian conspiracy and promised to send the *commentarii* for it.[2] Lucceius agreed, the *commentarii* were sent, but the *historia* was not written.[3] Cicero's *commentarius consulatus sui* was, indeed, no ordinary *commentarius*. He writes thus to Atticus, who also had written a *commentarius* on the same theme:

On the first of June I met your servant....He handed to me your letter and a *commentarius* on my consulship written in Greek. I am very glad that some time ago I gave to L. Cossinius to bring to you the book I had written on the same theme also in

[1] *ad Attic.* II, 1, 1–2.   [2] *ad Fam.* V, 12, 10.
[3] *ad Attic.* IV, 6, 4; IV, 11, 2.

Greek, for if I had read yours first you would say I had plagiarized from you. Though yours—while I enjoyed reading it—seemed to me a trifle rough and unkempt ('horridula atque incompta'), yet its neglect of adornment seemed an adornment in itself, and it was like women who were thought to have the best scent because they used none; whereas my book has used up all the unguents of Isocrates, all the perfumes of his pupils and a trace of Aristotelian cosmetics.

Cicero writes to his friend with a kind of apologetic self-irony. But he could not refrain from fine writing about what appeared to him, more clearly than to others, a fine subject, *consulatus suus*. And he was not deprived of free will by the convention of a literary form. But the traditional form for a *commentarius*, however far it had gone on the way to *historia*, was simple and matter-of-fact.

In 46 B.C. when Cicero wrote his *Brutus*, having read those at least of Caesar's *Commentaries* which treated of his exploits in Gaul, he said they were written 'that others might have material to their hand if they composed a *historia*'.[1] So far he is placing them in the category of commentaries that await transmutation into *historia*, but he adds a significant phrase 'so that Caesar may have seemed a benefactor to the foolish who wished to take the curling-tongs to them, but that sensible men were frightened off writing on the basis of them'. Cicero may have remembered the answer of Poseidonius,

[1] 75, 262.

and have laid a little flattering unction to his soul. So, too, Hirtius, in the preface to the Eighth Book of the *Gallic War*, says that Caesar's *Commentaries* have been published 'that *writers* might not lack knowledge of these great events', but he adds 'and they are so approved by all men's judgement'— 'ut praerepta, non praebita facultas scriptoribus videatur'. Cicero's verdict, echoed, we may suppose, by Hirtius, is that Caesar's writings have a quality which precludes attempts by others to do better what Caesar has done so well. His *Commentaries*, while they remain commentaries, have a literary eminence in their own right. When Cicero wrote the *Brutus* he was in a rare mood of hope of Caesar as a statesman, and the all-powerful dictator would read what he had written, but Cicero was an honest critic, a dictator himself in his own field, the field of letters, and it need not be doubted that he said what he thought. To him the *Commentaries* approach the literary finality appropriate to the finished product of *historia*. When he praises them— 'nudi enim sunt, recti et venusti, omni ornatu orationis tamquam veste detracta', he adds 'nihil est enim in *historia* pura et inlustri brevitate dulcius'. It would seem that this sensitive and instructed critic of letters believed, if only for a moment, that Caesar's *Commentaries* challenged *historia* on its own ground with comparable, if not identical, qualities.

When Caesar set out for Gaul he was not yet in

the first rank of generals, but he was an orator of an acknowledged eminence at a time when oratorical power was one hall-mark of literary distinction. Hortensius, the older rival of Cicero, had lost ground. Now, if Cicero was the first orator of Rome, Caesar was advancing to the second place until he found other things to do than to be an orator. Quintilian, who was fortunate enough to be able to read Caesar's speeches, says of his oratory 'si foro tantum vacasset, non alius ex nostris contra Ciceronem nominaretur', and adds, to justify his judgement, 'tanta in eo vis est, id acumen, ea concitatio, ut illum eodem animo dixisse quo bellavit appareat; exornat tamen haec omnia mira sermonis, cuius proprie studiosus fuit, elegantia'.[1] Caesar's force and vehemence, especially in his younger days, are well attested. For these qualities the manner of a *commentarius* offered little scope, though, as will be seen, they are at times discernible. But what Cicero praises as his 'pura et inlustris brevitas' could be attained by his 'mira sermonis elegantia'. The simplicity appropriate to the *commentarius* appealed to Caesar's literary predilections. As between the florid style of the Asianic school and the austere plain style of the Atticists Caesar was inclined to the Atticists, if not slavishly or to excess. His mentor in oratory had been Apollonius Molon of Rhodes, who set himself against the redundant Asianic style. It would be rash to assume that Caesar was not capable

[1] *Inst. Or.* X, I, 114.

14

of going his own way, but, granted that, Molon's teaching may well have been to his mind.

Another of his teachers was the grammarian Antonius Gnipho, who carried further a systematic purism inspired by the study of language and its forms that the Stoics had inaugurated, and aroused in Caesar an interest in linguistic niceties, especially in the forms of words. In 55 B.C. Cicero in his *De Oratore*[1] had taken these doctrines lightly and had claimed for an orator a freedom to follow general use without requiring the justification of what was called analogy which would dictate the forms of words by a kind of orthographical orthodoxy. It is a reasonable conjecture[2] that Caesar was moved to spend some leisure in the winter of 55/54 in writing his two books *De Analogia*, incidentally refuting Cicero's concessions to popular usage.

Whether or not in his commentaries Caesar insisted upon the orthographical forms of his analogistic theory it is hard to say. The MS. tradition, on the whole, suggests that he did not,[3] but MS. tradition is not a certain guide. He may, however, very well have supposed that a work like his *Commentaries* was not the place for theoretical niceties. His famous injunction to keep clear of 'inauditum atque insolens verbum' was doubtless directed against neologisms, but it may have

[1] III, 37, 150–38, 154.
[2] See G. L. Hendrickson in *Class. Philology*, I (1906), pp. 97 ff.
[3] See W. A. Oldfather and G. Bloom in *Class. Journ.* XXII (1927), pp. 584–602.

haunted him when it came to grammatical forms that had only theoretical justification. As Eduard Norden in his *Antike Kunstprosa* has shown, Latin had been becoming more systematic in structure and, at the same time, less luxuriant in vocabulary. To give Norden's illustration: in the second-century *de Bacchanalibus* of 186 B.C. four different words are used to mean 'conspiring together'— 'coniurare, convovere, conspondere, compromittere'. Of these four, only the first 'coniurare' remained in use with this meaning in the Ciceronian period. It is well known how Caesar seemed at times to have decided that a particular thing is most properly described by a particular word. For him a river is always 'flumen' and never 'fluvius' or 'amnis'. The economy of his style is in the new tradition of Latin— in Newman's phrase, 'always the right word for the right idea and never a word too much'. The simple brevity appropriate to the *commentarius* form did not preclude the exercise of Caesar's 'mira sermonis elegantia, cuius proprie studiosus fuit'.

The theme of Caesar's *Commentaries* is his *res gestae* and this fact brings in another element which is less objective than the older *commentarius*. It is autobiographical, or, if not that, descriptive of the events in which some eminent man had played a leading part. Great men had begun to write about their own doings in self-justification or to claim the form of immortality which Roman aristocrats prized, the memory of their services to the State. Like the

16

ecclesiastic who set up his epitaph in anticipation
of his demise, they thought it well to be their own
chroniclers. When Cicero wrote the *Brutus* he cited
two such works. One is that of M. Aemilius Scaurus
de vita sua;[1] the other, a book by C. Lutatius Catulus the elder, *de consulatu suo et de rebus gestis suis*,[2]
written 'molli et Xenophontio genere sermonis'.
Aemilius Scaurus had enjoyed more continuous
good fortune than good repute, and his work may
have been in part an 'apologia pro vita sua'.
Catulus's campaign in north Italy had been the
high light of his military career, though it was over-
shadowed by the exploits of his colleague Marius.
He dedicated his book to the poet A. Furius, and it
has been plausibly conjectured[3] that he hoped his
friend would write an epic on the Cimbrian War in
which his merits would be immortalized. Cicero
says that the works of Scaurus and Catulus were no
longer read in his day, but this is not to be taken
au pied de la lettre. The elder Pliny, Tacitus and
Valerius Maximus knew of Scaurus's autobiography,
and a reference in Frontinus is probably ultimately
derived from the same work. Two centuries later
Fronto speaks of certain *Epistulae* of Catulus which
are probably his dispatches to the Senate and
material for his book. More relevant were Sulla's
twenty-two books which, to judge from the ancient

---

[1] *Brutus*, 29, 112; Pliny, *N.H.* XXXIII, 21; Tacitus, *Agric.* 1, 3; Val.
Max. IV, 4, 11; Frontinus, *Strat.* IV, 3, 13.
[2] *Brutus*, 35, 132.   [3] H. Peter, *Hist. Rom. Rel.*[2], I, p. cclxv.

references, probably bore the title *L. Cornelii Sullae commentarii rerum gestarum*. It is plain from Plutarch's *Lives* of Marius and of Sulla that, as the dictator contemplated his rivals and enemies, he did not write 'sine ira et studio' and that when he wrote of himself he wrote *con amore*. It would be idle to suppose that in such works the author did not give himself the benefit of any doubt, or that when members of the high aristocracy of Rome read Caesar's *commentarii rerum gestarum* they imagined that their author had a disinterested desire to tell the truth, the whole truth, and nothing but the truth. This is a matter to be discussed later (pp. 22 ff.). It is enough to say at this point that the *res gestae* element has to be remembered in evaluating the composite literary character of Caesar's writings.

Finally, there is an ingredient in the composition of Caesar's works which affects alike their content and their style, and that is the personality of the author. Granted that Caesar was *omnium consensu* a skilful man of letters, he was more than that—he was a man endowed with a 'vivida vis animi', of singular determination and resource, ruefully admitted to be 'a portent of terrible vigilance, speed and application'.[1] Whatever the literary form which he employed, and however well he preserved its conventions, it was not possible that his personality should not be at times visible, so that his commentaries are a plain texture shot with genius.

[1] *ad Attic.* VIII, 9, 4.

2

THE PURPOSE AND CONTENT OF CAESAR'S 'COMMENTARIES'

I T is often said that Caesar had a purpose in writing his *Commentaries* and it is sometimes said, and more often implied, that his purpose was political or, at least, directly concerned with his own advancement. In an age in which publicity is the servant of policy and ambition it is natural for us to suppose that this would be so, and that Caesar would not neglect any means that helped found his own interests and the interests of whatever cause he wished to serve. If he has little to say about Roman politics except in self-justification at the outbreak of the Civil War, this may be regarded as the art that conceals art. Mr T. E. Page is credited with the dictum 'Caesar's *Gallic War* indeed—a subtle political pamphlet beginning with the words "All Gaul is divided into three parts"'. It is a hard saying, but it is not all the truth. There is in Caesar's writings an element of propaganda, but it is not predominant, and it is not what matters most.

Propaganda does not exist in a vacuum, and it is worth while to consider to whom the propaganda, what there is of it, was addressed. When Mommsen

2-2

declared that Caesar's *Commentaries* were the report of the democratic general to the People, he is expressing his view that Caesar was the democratic champion of the People against a blind or unworthy aristocracy. But this view does Caesar less or more than justice. He was ready to invoke the sovereignty of the People at need to overcome opposition if he could not achieve his ends, whether of personal ambition or of statesmanship, otherwise. But the voice of the People was to be an echo of his own. Like most Romans whose position made them stand for Rome, he sought the greatness of Rome against all comers. But he must have been aware that, for most of the time and in most matters, Rome was the Senate first and the People afterwards, if at all. The Senate was guided by consuls and consulars and might be hampered by tribunes. At elections all kinds of influences, reputable and disreputable, played upon the part of the electorate that voted. It was possible for tribunes to bring proposals before the Concilium Plebis, but what one tribune proposed another tribune could veto. And the Senate, by convention, settled many questions, especially the kind of questions that mattered most to a proconsul. The courts which might sit in judgement on his actions when he returned to Rome were manned by members of the upper classes, and from the decision of these courts there was no appeal. In the absence of an adequate police force, the progress of public affairs might at times be hampered or deflected by the riff-raff of the city. But the riff-raff of the city did not read books. The goodwill of the towns of Italy might be of value at elections or when some proposal was strengthened by the manifestation of a wide public opinion in its favour. But here too it was probably the local notables that counted, if they took the trouble to bring themselves and their clients to Rome. But, for most purposes at most times, public opinion was made by what senators said in the Senate or in private or wrote to their friends. Caesar was at pains to conduct a correspondence with men like Cicero, who in turn could influence this public opinion. He had a patronage that could help his friends and the friends of his friends. The wealth of rich men of the senatorial or equestrian order might be used for political ends, for votes in elections or in the courts might be bought. The governor of a province had to take account of financial interests established there so as not to offend rich men whose influence could do him harm. Caesar, in Gaul outside the old Province, had no old financial interests to consider but could help or hinder new ones. There were scattered over Italy men who had served under this general or that, though Caesar had not commanded large armies before he went to Gaul, and most of those who had served under him served with him still.

When all these things are borne in mind, and when it is remembered how small and slow would be the circulation of an ancient book, even granted that secondary circulation that comes from the diffusion of opinion by speech or private correspondence, Caesar must have known that, both for his present interests and his future reputation, he must write, primarily, for men of his own class and, above all, for the aristocracy of Rome which rated military skill and success more highly than anything else. Within his own army his influence, so far as it was not secured by the high military tradition and discipline of the legions, rested on success and the effect of his personality on his officers, from the *legati* downwards to the centurions in their hierarchical precedence of rank, and then on the legionaries themselves. The men of the Tenth Legion did not need to await the publication of a *commentarius* to know what Caesar thought of them and trusted them to achieve.

The moment when the most widespread effect was most needed was before an election to high office, and so the publication of the *Commentaries* may have preceded by several months the earliest moment at which Caesar may have contemplated becoming a candidate for his second consulship. But apart from any possible choice of the moment for publication, the writing of the *Commentaries*, if the view that this proceeded year by year is accepted, would have, in the main, the purpose of describing what happened as Caesar saw it, in part to satisfy a kind of intellectual appreciation of his own doings and that of others, in part to satisfy an interest in military technique which he shared with most men of his own class, the technique including a mastery over men as well as over things, and, finally, the promotion of his own *dignitas*, which is the acceptance of his claim to high office and public consideration and honours, to the opportunity to guide policy and be master of the event, and to the recognition of what he, and those who fought with him, had done to serve the greatness of Rome. He did not deny to the enemies of Rome the right to fight against her, and he did not seek to belittle or condemn them, if only because he would have done the same in their place. But he had inherited a tradition that taught him to maintain and extend the power of Rome, and he was ready to be judged by the extent to which he fulfilled that purpose. He did not need to convince himself of his own greatness; he sought to make it impossible for others to deny it, to underrate it or leave it unrewarded. This is, in a sense, propaganda, but to call Caesar's writings nothing else is to underrate alike their purpose and their quality.

It is to be remembered that, quite apart from any ulterior purpose that Caesar may have had, his *Commentaries* were bound to be subjective in the sense that they reveal events as Caesar saw them. The literary form, the content, the arrangement, the tradition of the *Commentaries*, cannot prevent their being so. Had Labienus written *Commentaries on the Gallic War* or Pompey *Commentaries on the Civil War*, they would have been different from

Caesar's writings in emphasis and interpretation. No man, however sincere, however content to let the facts speak for themselves, can describe great events in which he took a leading part with perfect objectivity. They become part of himself and are seen as he sees himself in his mirror, not as others may see them or as they may see him in action. And when a great man judges the action of his helpers or his antagonists he is bound to measure them by his own standards and to see them in relation to his own fortunes and purposes. Clear-sighted as Caesar was, in order to see things as they are, it is plain that they must be seen, as it were, *de haut en bas* from his self-confident intellectual eminence. The acts of other men, the way things turned out, are bound to be the raw material of his *res gestae*.

Caesar was above 'peacock tail-spreading vanity' as he was above 'hissing gander-like pride', but he had no doubt of his own greatness, and of his in-born right to it. He is not only adroit but wholly sincere when he writes to Cicero of himself and of his enemies: 'I desire nothing more than that I should be like myself—and they like themselves.' This does not mean that Caesar might not be high-handed with the factual truth, which was to him a good servant but a bad master. In the justification of his acts, to himself as to others, he may give himself the benefit of the doubt, and he was not scrupulous to his own hurt. If, for example, he sent a dispatch to the Senate which would make it hard for his enemies to cavil at his actions or condemn his purposes, what he aimed at writing then need not be the truth, the whole truth and nothing but the truth. And in his *Commentaries* he was not concerned to refute his dispatches.

1. THE FIRST BOOK OF THE GALLIC WAR

With this in mind, we may turn to the *Commentaries* to see what they contain which assists an understanding of how things looked to Caesar, and how, with his help, they look to others, and to ourselves. The effect of the *commentarius* form is perhaps most clearly to be discerned in the First Book of the *Gallic War*. The traditional form of the *commentarius* was concerned with events in isolation, each event being recorded, as it were, for its own sake. The more nearly a narrative approaches this traditional form the more it is a statement of acts and the less it is concerned with the interrelation of acts. Herein there may lie an economy of the truth, conscious or unconscious. The main theme of the First Book of the *Gallic War* is twofold: first the operations of Caesar against the Helvetii, which lead to their defeat, second the operations of Caesar against the German Ariovistus, which lead to his defeat. Each of these is a war in its own right, in each of these Caesar is the prime agent, and thus the *res gestae* or autobiographical element in the *Commen-*

taries finds expression. The story of each series of operations is told with matter-of-fact brevity, with an unadorned precision of phrasing that suited Caesar's literary predilections, as it suited the traditional manner of a *commentarius*.

Many scholars have been critical of the First Book as a witness of truth. They have no other comparable ancient account to use as a control; Cicero's letters give no help. The military events were known to Caesar's officers, and must have been, if only briefly, reported to the Senate in accordance with the standard practice of proconsuls. There was, it is true, a tradition which declared that the defeat of the Tigurini, who were caught on the wrong side of the river Arar, was the exploit not of Caesar but of Labienus.[1] This tradition, however, appears to go back to Labienus himself, who is not an impartial witness. It is not difficult to suppose that Labienus, who often led the cavalry, began the attack on Caesar's instructions, and that Caesar with three legions came up and finished it. He may have omitted to mention Labienus's share in what he represents as, in fact, a kind of family revenge for the killing by the Tigurini of his father-in-law's grandfather, L. Piso, half a century before.[2] Caesar does not fail to give due credit to his *legati* where they are acting as independent commanders, and the incident does

[1] Plutarch, *Caesar*, 18, 1; Appian, *Celt.* 1, 3, and xv; Dio Cassius xxxviii, 32, 4; Caesar and Dio Cassius do not mention Labienus.
[2] *B.G.* 1, 12, 7.

not make his account of military events suspect. Like most generals, Caesar, consciously or not, exaggerated the numbers of the enemy or their losses; he may have concealed mistakes, but he does not conceal the fact that the final battle with the Helvetii might well have gone the other way—'ita ancipiti proelio diu atque acriter pugnatum est'[1]— or that the battle against Ariovistus was restored by the timely action of the young P. Crassus.[2] He does not allege that when he turned away from following the Helvetii he hoped that they would be induced to give him the opportunity of fighting them on favourable ground, as they did.

There is no doubt that Caesar took considerable risks and that he could have protected the Roman province without attacking the Helvetii, and that the immediate interests of Rome did not require Caesar to take so strong a line with Ariovistus. The *commentarius* form makes it natural to keep Caesar's dealings with the Helvetii and Ariovistus separate and, as *res gestae*, they are just two successive exploits. But is that, or need that be, all the truth? For example, when Caesar had denied to the Helvetii a passage through the province, could he not have arranged with Ariovistus, whom he had caused to be recognized as the Friend of the Roman People, that the Sequani should be told not to open to the emigrants the pass through their territory, which Caesar says was easily defensible? The Sequani would not

[1] *B.G.* I, 26, I.   [2] *B.G.* I, 52, 7.

27

have dared to disobey. The Helvetii might have abandoned their project, or if they took, as they might, a more northerly route, they would pass through territory towards which Rome had no obligations. The Gauls, reinforced by the immigration of the Helvetii and their allies, might perhaps make head against the Germans, and Roman interests would, for the present at least, be secure without any exertions on Rome's part. That would be a quite traditional process of Roman statecraft. In any event, an alliance between Gauls and Germans might seem highly improbable. There are, in fact, various policies which Caesar might have adopted if his object had been limited to preserving existing Roman interests and showing some consideration for the friends and allies of Rome including 'their brothers, the Aedui'.

How far Caesar was conscious of these possibilities it is hard to say: the *commentarius* form does not at least bring them to the notice of his readers. It suits Caesar's drastic methods to act as he did. Another proconsul might have acted otherwise, though when there had been an alarm at Rome in March 60 B.C. and the consul Metellus Celer had been marked out to be the next proconsul in Transalpine Gaul, Cicero says that he was disappointed when the alarm came to nothing, for he was dreaming of a triumph.[1] It may be that war with the Helvetii was certain because it was the first war in

[1] *ad Attic.* I, 20, 5.

Gaul which Caesar could find ready to his hand. Caesar does not need to say this, if we may assume it to be true. What he does say is that Rome did not allow barbarians to cross one of their provinces. He reminds his future readers of the last immigration, with the dangers it brought, fifty years before, and he says: 'Caesar non exspectandum sibi statuit, dum omnibus fortunis sociorum consumptis in Santonos Helvetii pervenirent.'[1] He passed beyond the province and attacked. In the end he defeats the Helvetii and compels (and allows) the major part of them and their allies to return to their homes so as not to produce a vacuum into which Germans might be drawn and so come dangerously near to the Roman province.

The communities of Central Gaul were impressed by Caesar's victory. They had suffered, or they feared to suffer, from Ariovistus with his growing power reinforced by relays of Germans from across the Rhine. There is no reason to doubt that the pro-Roman leader of the Aedui, Diviciacus, who had sought the help of the Senate two years before, now sought the help of Caesar. The formulation of his hopes—'Caesarem vel auctoritate sua atque exercitus [vel] recenti victoria vel nomine populi Romani deterrere posse ne maior multitudo Germanorum Rhenum traducatur, Galliamque omnem ab Ariovisti iniuria posse defendere'[2]—may been have prearranged. It was the springboard for Caesar's next

[1] *B.G.* I, 11, 6.   [2] *B.G.* I, 31, 16.

leap. Caesar assured the Gallic notables 'magnam se habere spem, et beneficio suo et auctoritate adductum Ariovistum finem iniuriis facturum'.[1] He then sets out a series of considerations which, he says, moved him 'ad eam rem cogitandam et suscipiendam'. They are in terms suited to Roman interests, pride and fears, the old fears that had haunted Rome since the days of the Cimbri and Teutoni and even longer—'quibus rebus quam maturrime occurrendum putabat'. They may, indeed, reflect the kind of thing Caesar wrote when he reported to the Senate the inception of this enterprise after it had succeeded. He adds the revealing sentence: 'Ipse autem Ariovistus tantos sibi spiritus, tantam adrogantiam sumpserat, ut ferendus non videretur.' This reflects his belief that, in fact, the only settlement would be by war. He believed he knew his Ariovistus and he was sure he knew himself. With a firm hand he guided the negotiations that followed to their destined end.

At this point, as in his account of the incipient mutiny at Vesontio and his handling of it, his personality becomes dominant. He appears to believe that Ariovistus may come to a peaceful settlement, though he has good grounds for confidence if he does not. 'Denique hos esse eosdem quibuscum saepe numero Helvetii congressi non solum in suis sed etiam in illorum finibus plerumque superarint, qui tamen pares esse nostro exercitui non potuerint.'[2]

[1] *B.G.* I, 33, 1.   [2] *B.G.* I, 40, 7.

So Napoleon, in a Caesarian moment: 'ces mêmes Prussiens qui sont aujourd'hui si vantards étaient à 3 contre 1 à Jéna et à 9 contre 1 à Montmirail'. In what follows Caesar displays his eminent under-standing of the art of being a soldier's general, an art that never deserted him. There is no reason to doubt the essential truth of his report of his speech,[1] least of all of its famous close: 'Quod si praeterea nemo sequatur, tamen se cum sola decima legione iturum, de qua non dubitet, sibique eam praetoriam cohortem futuram.' All this shows how in Caesar's hands the *commentarius* form could be made to con-vey the revelation of his own personality in the easy mastery of men. There is no rhetoric, and the note is not forced. Caesar was speaking to his aristocratic officers, and all his centurions, not only those seniors who normally attended his *consilium*, and to a larger audience, those Romans who had an ingrained instinct for war and an ingrained respect for those who understood the lessons of that hard teacher. And he knew what the men of the Tenth Legion would say when their centurions passed the word round. His army fought well when it came to fighting, and Ariovistus was decisively defeated. A remnant of his forces escaped across the Rhine, and the Suebi who had gathered on the river began to return to their homes.

Much has been made of the fact that the same

---

[1] Its truth is not challenged by Plutarch, *Caesar*, 19, or by the long harangue composed by Dio Cassius, XXXVIII, 36–46.

Caesar who as consul had caused Ariovistus to be declared the Friend of the Roman People, as proconsul marched against him. It is not known when in his consulship the title was conferred, whether before or after Caesar had Transalpine Gaul added to his *provincia* as proconsul. If it was before, and perhaps even if it was after, that event, Caesar may have been bribed, and that was all. He needed money and Rome needed friends—for so long as it needed them. If Ariovistus was not a subservient friend he was no friend at all: *amicus* was as *amicus* did. Orators existed to cloak this fact by fine words. Had Caesar been defeated by Ariovistus he might have been prosecuted for a blunder transmuted into a crime. What mattered was success. Success meant innocence, unless he was arraigned before a court to whom guilt or innocence was of no moment. Or the naming of Ariovistus as *amicus* was an indication of policy—to put him on an equality with the Aedui, the long-established 'brothers' of Rome, to be on with the new love before being off with the old. Whichever was the reason, the *amicitia* of Ariovistus was a debating point in debate (as Caesar made it)[1] and to the Romans a standard of conduct for Ariovistus: to Ariovistus a standard of conduct for Rome, but Caesar had not to satisfy Ariovistus but Rome, and late Republican Rome judged Romans by success, if it judged by any standard at all. How greatly the Senate was concerned about the

[1] *B.G.* I, 43.

German peril is a matter of conjecture, but its elimination, if only temporary, meant one complication the less in a world that had been becoming inconveniently more complicated for more than a generation. Whenever Caesar wrote his account of the year 58, the events of that year, taken by themselves, were an asset and not a liability in his balance sheet as it stood when that year closed—'una aestate duobus maximis bellis confectis.'[1]

2. THE SECOND BOOK

Even before the autumn of 58 B.C. had ended, Caesar put his legions into winter quarters in the territory of the Sequani, most probably in and around the *place d'armes* of Vesontio (Besançon). He retired to his other province of Cisalpine Gaul, to the peaceful jurisdiction of a Roman governor. What reasons he gave to the Senate, if he gave any, for stationing his army outside his own province, he does not reveal. The effect was to produce a hostile reaction among the great confederacy of the Belgae, whom he had described as the most warlike people of Gaul.[2] The news of this was sent to him, and he raised two more legions this side the Alps and returned to his army when the season was far enough advanced to ease his supplies of food and the Belgae had time to prepare to take the field. The disunions that afflicted the national movement brought to the

[1] *B.G.* I, 54, 2.   [2] *B.G.* I, 1, 2.

side of Rome the Remi, 'qui dicerent se suaque omnia in fidem atque potestatem populi Romani permittere neque se cum Belgis reliquis consensisse neque contra populum Romanum coniurasse'.[1] All was in order: there was a *coniuratio* of enemies of Rome; Germans this side the Rhine had joined the Belgae; and there were new subjects to protect. By wariness alternating with vigour Caesar caused the enemy concentration to break up and attacked the tribes piecemeal. For a time all went according to plan, but he was surprised by the Nervii and only just won one of the hardest battles of his career. 'That day he overcame the Nervii.' His account will be analysed in a later chapter (pp. 69 f.). He claimed the almost complete destruction of the Nervii, and went on to deal with the Atuatuci, whose chief town was taken after they had broken the terms of a capitulation. More than fifty thousand inhabitants were sold into slavery. The campaign was a typically Roman combination of diplomatic reasonableness and military ruthlessness, which to Romans justified itself by its success. Caesar had sent the young Publius Crassus with a legion to south-west Gaul and news came that the tribes of the Atlantic seaboard had submitted to Roman power. The report proved, in the end, optimistic, but it served Caesar's purpose. Tribes beyond the Rhine, so he says, sent envoys promising to give hostages and to obey his commands, and he bade them send again at the begin-

[1] *B.G.* II, 3, 2.

ning of the next summer, as he was in a hurry to go to northern Italy and Illyricum.[1] He sent a dispatch to the Senate whereupon 'a public thanksgiving of fifteen days was decreed for his achievements—a greater honour than had previously been granted to anyone'.[2]

3. THE THIRD BOOK

So ends the Second Book with a fanfare of triumph. Events were to show that Caesar was making a large overdraft on his military credit. He may have included in his letter to the Senate that he was sending Servius Galba with a legion and some cavalry to open up the route across the Alps, wintering in the mountains if he thought it needful. Galba failed to achieve this object, and after a hard-won defensive battle withdrew to the Roman province.[3]

How far Caesar may have deceived himself about the position in Gaul it is hard to say. It was perhaps reasonable for him to suppose, as he says, that Gaul was pacified, at least in the sense that it contained no people who were in arms against Rome, so that the Roman province beyond the Alps was secure. He was responsible for Illyricum, and set out to acquaint himself with that region when news came that the Roman peace was broken. The maritime Veneti on the west coast of Gaul had started a strong reaction, and had taken Roman officers to exchange

[1] *B.G.* II, 35, 1–2.   [2] *B.G.* II, 35, 4.   [3] *B.G.* III, 1–6.

against the hostages they had given to Publius
Crassus. Whatever Caesar may have thought before,
he realized that the Gauls feared to be reduced to
subjection: 'they were easily provoked to war, and
all men naturally love freedom and hate servitude'.[1]
The Veneti were ringed round with armies, and
Caesar himself marched against them. A fleet was
built, and a victory at sea ended the hopes of the
Veneti, who surrendered at discretion. They had
loved freedom beyond their means. Their council-
lors were executed and the rest of the population
were sold as slaves. Even so, not all Gaul was
'pacified', for the coastal tribes of the Morini and
Menapii between the Somme and the Rhine remained in arms. There was only enough summer left
for a short campaign, and Caesar was not able to
solve the military problems presented by the
forests and marshes into which the enemy could
retire and take refuge.

Caesar had no doubt reported to the Senate his
action against the Veneti and his own success and
that of his lieutenants. But, at the most, he had only
made truer the claim of the previous year that Gaul
was pacified and he has nothing to say of a thanksgiving granted to him. It is possible that he was
beginning to believe that the Gallic problem did not
end with Gaul. During the year 56 his political
position had been secured by a renewed agreement
with Pompey and Crassus, and his command in

[1] *B.G.* III, 10, 3.

Gaul had been prolonged to last until 50 B.C. if not later. Thus Caesar could pursue long plans as proconsul if he wished to do so, and bring Germany and Britain within his calculations. The next year was in fact to contain three events: the sharp repulse of a German invasion, and two reconnaissances, the one across the Rhine, the other across the English Channel.

4. THE FOURTH BOOK

In 58 B.C. Caesar had driven the German Ariovistus out of Gaul. During the winter of 56/55 he became aware that a new invasion of Gaul was happening and that behind the invasion, and indeed the cause of it, there was the dangerous power of the Suebi, 'the most numerous and most warlike of the German peoples'.[1] He explains that they had driven from their homes two tribes, the Usipetes and Tencteri, who in the end had crossed the lower Rhine into Gallic territory to find lands to settle. He took the field earlier than usual, marched against them and destroyed them by trickery and the merciless use of force. He then decided to bridge the Rhine and enter Germany. He explains his motives: he wished to deter further German aggression by showing that the Romans were able and ready to cross the river, to impress this fact on the Sugambri on the right bank, and to encourage the Ubii, who had sought Roman protection, to believe that, with

[1] B.G. IV, 1, 3.

37

Roman help at need, they could maintain themselves against the Suebi.[1] In the course of eighteen days he ravaged the country of the Sugambri, displayed his legions to the Ubii, and returned to Gaul, destroying the bridge behind him. But he did not venture to advance far enough to give battle to the Suebi, who had concentrated far back in their territory and left to him an empty country to march across. Caesar declared that he had achieved all his objects.

Then, though summer was near its end, Caesar carried out a brief invasion of Britain. He says that in almost all the campaigns in Gaul the Britons had sent help to his enemies, and that it would be an advantage to become acquainted with the land, harbours and landing-places, for of all these the Gauls knew hardly anything.[2] The British help to the Gauls and the Gallic ignorance of Britain are not beyond doubt. That Caesar wished to see what could be done about a serious invasion of Britain is probable enough. There may have been another reason, to make an effect on Roman society. Cicero in his speech on the consular provinces, delivered in 56, had proclaimed not only the conquest of the old enemies of Rome but the opening of new regions of the earth.[3] The admirers of Pompey had dilated on his achievements in the East in like terms a decade before. Germany was still *terra incognita*, and Britain was near the world's end, and stretched into

---

[1] *B.G.* IV, 16.   [2] *B.G.* IV, 20, 1–2.
[3] 13, 33; see also Catullus, 11, 9–12.

mystery. The Romans, so far as they were explorers, had explored sword in hand, and if Caesar's main purposes were military rather than tinged with the spirit of inquiry that had been a part of Alexander's expedition to India, he might well have in mind the impression his enterprises might produce. Neither the demonstration into Germany nor the reconnaissance into Britain meant any significant extension of Roman power, but they had their effect, and on the news of them the Senate decreed a further thanksgiving of twenty days. And during the winter great preparations were made to carry a larger army to Britain in the next year (54 B.C.).

5. THE FIFTH BOOK

In Gaul itself Caesar had sought to increase the influence of the Aedui, the old allies of Rome, and to advance the local power of chieftains whom he believed he could trust. In doing so he had incurred the hostility of Indutiomarus, an able and determined chief among the Treveri. Gallic notables were to accompany the Roman army to Britain as hostages for the good behaviour of their communities, and when the Aeduan chief Dumnorix tried to escape he was pursued and killed. It was becoming plain that the best the Gallic leaders could expect was to be the clients of Rome. Although an army of three legions under Labienus watched Roman interests in Gaul, Caesar campaigned in Britain with the knowledge that he must not stay too long. The south-eastern Britons had found an able leader in Cassivelaunus, who led the national resistance until Caesar was content to admit him to a surrender which was complete enough to protect Roman prestige. And that was all. Caesar returned to the continent.

The enterprise, for all the skill and fighting power displayed in the campaign, had proved a doubtful investment of Caesar's military strength. For when Caesar returned and held a council of Gallic leaders at Samarobriva he had cause for anxiety. He distributed his legions in a wide arc in north-eastern Gaul. The reason he gave for this distribution was that there had been a poor harvest and this was the best way of securing his supplies of corn for the winter. But when he says that no two legions were more than a hundred miles apart except one that was in a perfectly peaceful district he gives a hint of danger, and he determined to stay at hand until all the legions had fortified their appointed positions. Whatever his fears, they were justified. A widespread revolt had been planned by Indutiomarus and the first blow was struck by the Eburones under an able and relentless leader, Ambiorix. A Roman army of a legion and five cohorts under his lieutenants Sabinus and Cotta was lured out of its camp and destroyed almost to a man. The Nervii, in numbers that refute Caesar's claim that he almost destroyed them three years before, attacked the camp of Quintus Cicero. He was invited to march out into safety. But he was not to be tricked and held out stoutly. How dangerous the situation was may be seen from the fact that no word had reached Caesar until a slave sent by Cicero got through to him with an appeal for help. His chief lieutenant, Labienus, was pinned down by the Treveri. Acting with great speed and resource Caesar marched to the relief of Cicero just in time. It had been a near run thing and, all that winter, Caesar stayed in Gaul beset with anxieties. Only the Aedui and the Remi could be trusted. The general readiness to revolt was, Caesar says, not so surprising: among many other reasons, it was natural that tribes, considered the bravest and most warlike of mankind, should resent bitterly the complete loss of this reputation which submission to the rule of Rome entailed.[1]

Whereas in the third and fourth years of his governorship of Gaul Caesar appears to have the initiative, with the winter of the fourth to fifth year he is really on the defensive. Rome had two formidable and enterprising enemies, Indutiomarus and Ambiorix, and Labienus skilfully drew Indutiomarus within his reach and killed him—'Fortune justified the plan that human foresight had devised.'[2] This success made Gaul somewhat quieter for the time being. Three legions were raised to do more than replace the loss of the army of Sabinus and Cotta. 'This large and rapid reinforcement showed what Rome's organization and resources could accomplish.'[3]

[1] *B.G.* v, 54, 5.   [2] *B.G.* v, 58, 6.   [3] *B.G.* VI, 1, 3.

6. THE SIXTH BOOK

In 53 B.C. Caesar himself took the field before the normal campaigning season began, and re-established Rome's control of central Gaul. Labienus reduced the Treveri to submission, and set up a loyal chieftain to rule over them. There remained Ambiorix, and Caesar was concerned to prevent his receiving help from the Menapii, who had so far shown no signs of submitting to Rome, and from Germans beyond the Rhine. He swept through the country of the Menapii and then decided to cross the Rhine for a second time. But, once more, he did not feel able to advance so far as to bring the Suebi to battle, and once more he retired, though he left part of the bridge standing to show that he might return to the German side of the river.

Then came the systematic devastation of the country of Ambiorix, the attempt to make a solitude so as to call it peace. A general invitation to all comers to plunder the territory of the Eburones was accepted by 200 horsemen of the Sugambri, who then were tempted to try their luck in a surprise attack on Q. Cicero at Atuatuca, where he guarded the *impedimenta* of Caesar's army. The surprise was all but successful; Cicero had become careless and the recruits he had with him were seized with panic: indeed, only the bravery of the centurions and some veterans prevented a serious disaster. Caesar complained that fortune played him false,[1] and all the efforts he made to capture Ambiorix just missed success. He executed a Gallic chief who had plotted a revolt and outlawed others who had not waited to be tried. Two legions were posted among the Treveri, two others among the Lingones, and the remaining six were left concentrated in central Gaul. It is clear from the dispositions that Caesar was ill at ease, but he returned to Italy for the winter 'as he had planned to do'.[2]

7. THE SEVENTH BOOK

The book which follows is the climax of Caesar's own *Commentaries on the Gallic War*. It begins with the words 'Quieta Gallia', and goes on to present a chronicle of dangers which taxed Caesar's skill and courage as never before. So far as the first two words justify his absence south of the Alps 'as he had determined', the justification is submerged by a vivid account of the widespread resentment at the loss of Gallic freedom, of the hopes aroused by his presumed preoccupation with a political crisis at Rome, of the progress made by the national movement under a new leader before the news reached Caesar, of his perplexities and the risks he had to run to rejoin the army, so that with all his speed and resource it was hard to brave winter and his enemies with success. The striking compliment which he was

[1] *B.G.* VI, 43, 4.　　　　　[2] *B.G.* VI, 44, 3.

to pay to his lieutenant Labienus, 'tantis subito difficultatibus obiectis ab animi virtute auxilium petendum videbat',[1] gives the essence of his own reaction to these perplexities.

While the fighting strength of his army was at its zenith, Gaul had become a sea of enemies; the friends of Rome were few, and their loyalty was precarious. The faithful Commius[2] even deserted his fidelity, the disunion of the Gauls was transmuted into a good measure of unity under Vercingetorix, the leader of the Arverni; a people who, a generation before, had held the primacy of Gaul, a general able to organize for victory and to rise superior to reverses. Caesar had pursued the traditional Roman policy of promoting friends of Rome and trusting to client princes and above all to the power of the Aedui: in this crisis the policy became a liability rather than an asset. The season did not admit of the rapid movements that might have daunted the insurgents, the siege of Avaricum succeeded but at the cost of twenty-seven precious days. The siege of Gergovia was ended by a reverse which Caesar comes short of dissembling by saying that his troops overran his own discretion, if even that is true. For all the vigour of Caesar and Labienus, it seemed impossible to grasp and retain the initiative, to bring about a decisive battle under favourable conditions.

The narrative moves with urgent, almost anxious

[1] *B.G.* VII, 59, 6.   [2] See below, p. 79.

speed. The defensive system which rested on hostages kept in the territory of the Aedui breaks down when they take the field against the Romans, and it looks as though the great adventure of the conquest of Gaul might end in failure. The Roman province has to be rapidly organized for defence and Caesar, surrounded by enemies, has to put out all his skill to find a way of restoring the military situation. Vercingetorix suffers a reverse and retires on Alesia, and Caesar risks all on the hazard of besieging him, while the Gauls raise a great army which might hope to destroy the legions. For if Caesar's defence against them failed, it was the end of him and his whole army. Had this happened it is hard to see how the province could have weathered the storm, and how nearly it happened is plain from his narrative. The climax of the battle is reached; the fighting qualities of the legions, the vigour and courage of Caesar himself achieve victory. Vercingetorix surrenders, and the campaign ends with the Roman forces disposed to make good the control of central Gaul. The last of Caesar's own *Commentaries* on Gaul ends with the news reaching the Senate and the voting of a final *supplicatio*. Caesar himself winters at Bibracte for he knows that he is needed. His lieutenant Hirtius, who describes the events of the next two years in the Eighth Book of the *Commentaries* begins his book with the words 'Omni Gallia devicta'. The rest of that book shows how much has still to be done to make those words wholly true.

But for whatever reason, Caesar is content to end his own story of his achievements in Gaul with the crowning mercy of Alesia.

8. THE 'CIVIL WAR'

When we turn to the *Civil War*, it is noticeable that it begins with the first day of a Roman year by the current calendar. For that is the day on which the first event mentioned occurred. The first two books cover roughly the events of the year 49 and between them made up one *Commentarius*. But some scattered operations which happened in this year are brought into the Third Book, so that the strict division of *commentarii* by years is not preserved any more than between the second and third books of the *Gallic War* (p. 35). In the earlier chapters of Book I Caesar presents his case as regards the political and constitutional aspect of the outbreak of the war. Caesar is an advocate for himself, not wholly scrupulous, but wholly sincere. It is plain that he believed that he had not received the treatment which his exploits and his *dignitas* deserved, and that his army shared his belief. He did not seek to overthrow the Republican constitution, but only to have it work for his interests and not against them. He was prepared to meet his enemies at least part of the way provided he did not forfeit his career, to come to terms with Pompey in a new coalition in which, however, he would be at an advantage over his former ally. The *civilis dissensio* need not be a *bellum civile*; it was not by his choosing that his enemies made it one. As he said at Pharsalus, 'they would have it so'—'hoc voluerunt'.[1] The exposition is subtly contrived so as to be built up partly of what he said and did and what his opponents said and did, but it does not attain an objectivity in which no one could believe.

The military operations are militarily discussed with a cool evaluation of the application of *ratio belli* by both sides. It is taken for granted that Caesar would not sacrifice any military advantage to assist negotiations, and that his enemies would take the same line. But Caesar was anxious to show clemency where he could safely do so, to avoid bloodshed if he could advance his ends without it. The folly of Domitius Ahenobarbus at Corfinium, the pessimism of Afranius, the brutal violence of Petreius, the vacillation of Varro, the bad faith of the Massiliotes, the timidity of Varus, are revealed, but so far there is nothing that would embitter the conflict past reconciliation. There is no triumph over Pompey at his withdrawal from Italy, which Caesar no doubt judged more justly than Cicero, who complained of it, as though he understood war. There is not even a reference to the desertion of Labienus, though the fact that he was now in the opposite camp might be deduced from an incidental remark.[2] The support given by Juba of Numidia to his enemies in Africa is, in a way, justified.[3]

[1] Suetonius, *Divus Iulius*, 30, 4. [2] *B.C.* I, 15, 2. [3] *B.C.* II, 25, 4.

47

The Third Book strikes a sharper note. Metellus, Scipio, Labienus, Bibulus are attacked, the thwarting of Caesar's efforts to find a way to peace by the violence of Labienus, the egotistical ambition, the partisan hatreds, the unreasoning self-confidence of the nobles are portrayed. The skill of Pompey is not denied, but the break-down of his spirit when his plan miscarried at Pharsalus is revealed— 'summae rei diffidens et tamen eventum exspectans'.[1] The death of Pompey is recorded curtly after a phrase in which some critics have seen a touch of irony.[2] The book seems to reflect the anxieties that beset Caesar, the strain on his troops and the courage which both needed until the victory at Pharsalus and then the reaction to triumphant self-confidence 'confisus fama rerum gestarum' which made him believe everywhere was safe for him.[3] The anger of Caesar at finding himself in danger from the *soldateska* of Achillas and from the intrigues of Pothinus glows in the closing chapters of the book, which ends abruptly. If Caesar wrote the last words 'This was the beginning of the war of Alexandria' they seem to dismiss a topic beneath the level of Caesar's attention. It has been suggested[4] that the statement of the preceding sentence that he put Pothinus to death is a kind of

[1] *B.C.* III, 94, 6.
[2] *B.C.* III, 104, 3: 'naviculam parvulam conscendit cum paucis suis; ibi ab Achilla et Septimio interficitur.'
[3] *B.C.* III, 106, 3.
[4] By K. Barwick in *Philologus, Suppl.* XXXII, 2, p. 133f.

dramatic ending with the avenging of Pompey, but that is an over-subtlety and to the matter-of-fact Romans Pompey would not be avenged while his assassins, Achillas and Septimius, lived. The *Commentarius* does not contain all the history of the year's operations, and it remains, for whatever reason, formally incomplete.

3

THE 'MILITARY MAN'

ACCORDING to Plutarch[1] Caesar disclaimed rivalry with Cicero by describing himself as a 'military man'. There is self-irony in this: Caesar was well aware that he was not an inarticulate soldier: as an orator he enjoyed, in his own day and afterwards, a high reputation. Even if his grammatical work *De Analogia* was not written, as Fronto said, 'inter volantia pila', it showed a scholarly interest in linguistic forms which diversified his application to the business of a general and a governor. He had followed literary fashions in writing verse and his *Anticato*, if it was not worthy of his magnanimity, was an adventure in a field in which he had to stand comparison with eminent figures in Greek and Roman literature who had written such diatribes. The style of the *Commentaries* will be discussed later. It is enough for the moment to say that they possess qualities which prove that Caesar was an eminent writer.

Granted this, Caesar's main theme is military, the conduct of warfare by the Romans against Gauls, Germans and Britons and then against the Roman generals and the armies of his opponents in the Civil War. The topic does not fire the imagination,

[1] *Caesar*, 3, 4.

or win the sympathy, of a modern reader. The conquest of Gaul has a certain long-range historical
justification or partial justification. It can be argued
that the Gauls, divided among themselves and half-
way between the native valour of barbarism and the
military sophistication of civilization, could not have
saved themselves from German invaders, and that
subjection to Rome brought to the country much
peace, culture and prosperity. But these blessings
in the long run did not alleviate the lot of those who
were killed, bereaved, enslaved or plundered in the
short run. The Civil War and the conflict in Spain
that ended at Munda revealed some loyalty to a cause
and a great deal of loyalty to generals, but it is hard
to find inspiration in a struggle which neither side
wholly deserved to win. It is possible to maintain that
the Civil War was a stage on the way to the Principate, and easy to maintain that the Principate was
on balance a great blessing for the human race. But
civil war was not the only way, and was not the best
way. Rome could have been great and beneficent
without it, had there been more wisdom, more generosity, more of that valuable ingredient in human
affairs, simple 'give and take'.

Such reflections as these are in themselves salu-
tary, but the intellectual interest of the *Commentaries* is not greatly impaired by their validity. Whatever the purposes and whatever the effects of
Caesar's soldiering, his account of his doings and
those of his lieutenants and his antagonists repays

study. He was operating with troops of very high quality, of great steadiness and courage that increased as years of service under able centurions taught them to have faith in themselves and in their commanders. A veteran legion acquired a robust *esprit de corps*, like that of Napoleon's Old Guard or a famous regiment in a modern army. Now and again, especially among the least experienced troops, there was a failure of nerve, an access of panic such as may befall any army. Caesar himself may have had moments of dismay such as visited the stout-hearted Aemilius Paullus as he saw the Macedonian phalanx bear down on his army at Pydna.[1] But these moments are not revealed in the *Commentaries*, and, if they happened, they must have quickly passed. Caesar possessed that serene courage which was the outstanding characteristic of Marlborough and Wellington, and he expected it of his lieutenants and of his men and inspired it in them.

But to Caesar the conduct of war was, above all, an exercise of the mind—what he calls *ratio belli*—which must not be clouded by over-confidence or by under-confidence. When he went to Gaul he had comparatively little experience as a general and he had something to learn before he attained what the soldier who wrote the *Bellum Africum* calls his *mirabilis scientia bellandi*.[2] When he had attained this skill he was tempted to indulge the use of it

[1] Plutarch, *Aemilius*, 19, 2.   [2] *B. Afr.* 31, 4.

where something less might have sufficed. But he did not make a mystery of war. He assumes in his readers a general knowledge of the normal methods of Roman war, of the organization of units and their tactical use. Where some unusual military problem presented itself, as the bridging of a broad, deep and swiftly-flowing river,[1] or the landing of an army on a hostile coast in tidal conditions unknown in the Mediterranean,[2] he is at pains to explain how such problems were solved. The bridge over the Rhine was presumably devised by his engineers, but Caesar is interested to describe the problem and its solution —as it were for its own sake—'rationem pontis hanc instituit'. In the siege of Massilia his lieutenant Trebonius was faced by a problem of siegecraft in the construction of a tower. It was a problem, and the problem was solved: 'Id hac ratione perfectum est.'[3] An elaborate description is given of the construction and then of the logical exploitation of its advantages in the driving of a covered gallery to undermine the city wall. This achievement did not, in fact, cause the fall of the city, for the Massiliotes, by treachery, and aided by a storm, destroyed what had been built. But, though the tower and the gallery perished, it seems to Caesar worth while to give this description, perhaps, in fact, to do justice to the ingenuity of Trebonius and his engineers. But it shows how Caesar expects his readers

[1] *B.G.* IV, 17.   [2] *B.G.* V, I.
[3] *B.C.* II, 8 ff.

to have his own interest in a practical problem of the art of war.

These instances illustrate one side of Caesar's intellectual approach to war, the overcoming of material difficulties, the triumph of mind over matter. By the side of this may be set his appreciation and criticism of the human factors in war, both general and particular. In the *Gallic War* he rarely indicates any judgement of the military skill of enemy leaders. His direct praise is reserved for the 'magnitudo animi' of the barbarians which 'facilia ex difficillimis redegerat',[1] a triumph of courage. The course of the operations against Ariovistus justifies respect for the German as a strategist, but Caesar is concerned to stress his arrogance rather than his skill.[2] In the battle against the Nervii, their leader Boduognatus, is quick to seize a tactical advantage, and this can be deduced from the account. Indutiomarus, Ambiorix and Cassivelaunus in their different ways appear formidable; the figure of Vercingetorix stands out clear in the Seventh Book.

Vercingetorix is the most Caesarian of all Caesar's antagonists. He has the insight to detect the strategy that offers the best chance of success and the resolute authority which could impose it upon his countrymen. He can be ruthless and does not hesitate to resort to trickery to reassert himself after a reverse;[3] he contrives at least to initiate a move-

[1] *B.G.* II, 27, 5.　　　[2] *B.G.* I, 33, 5; 44, 1; 46, 4.
[3] *B.G.* VII, 20, 8-11.

ment of defection among the Aedui which de-
stroys the results of Roman policy in Central Gaul,
and, after the Roman reverse before Gergovia, to
which he may have tempted the legions, he imposes
on Caesar a hard choice between courses either of
which was bound to be dangerous, a choice of evils.
All this appears in Caesar's narrative without ex-
tenuation or apology. The appreciation of the military position which Vercingetorix is made to give
in *B.G.* VII, 66 marks a crisis. His calculations are
sound except that he does not know that Caesar has
procured cavalry and light-armed troops from
Germany. In chapter 67 their intervention at the
right moment turns the well-laid scheme of Vercingetorix into a disaster. He withdraws into
Alesia. Caesar does not say whether he regards this
step as a mistake. It may well have been the best
thing that Vercingetorix could have done, for there
are moments in war when 'bad is the best'. Granted
that the Gauls could not defeat Caesar's army in a
set battle, to besiege and at the same time to be
besieged, might overstrain the Roman forces in the
face of superior numbers, and it was in a siege, at
Gergovia, that Caesar had suffered his one serious
reverse. Caesar is concerned to show how well he
used his opportunity until the relieving army was
defeated and Alesia fell. In chapter 89 the case for
Vercingetorix is briefly stated. The rest of the chapter is the cold statement of the surrender. However
highly Caesar may have assessed the generalship and

personality of Vercingetorix, there was nothing to be gained by mercy, and eight years afterwards he walked in Caesar's triumph and was then executed.

Caesar is the *imperator*, his generals are his *legati*, his lieutenants only. Labienus called on his troops to fight as though the *imperator* was present.[1] In the *Civil War* Caesar, defending P. Sulla against the charge that he might have achieved victory, defines the duty of a *legatus*.[2] To Caesar the *res gestae* of his *legati* can be subsumed under his own *res gestae*, of which they are reckoned as a part. And his dispatches would presumably take that line. This does not hinder him from giving to them the fullest credit for their *consilia*, for their adherence to the *ratio belli*.[3] This is partly, perhaps, a desire to ensure their loyalty to him. It is true that until the close of the Gallic War his *legati* could hardly be anything else than loyal, but he knows that their belief in him is part of the general *esprit de corps* of his army. He is critical of Q. Cicero when in 53 B.C. he seems to doubt if Caesar would carry out his purposes.[4] Beneath the account of the discussions between Sabinus and Cotta[5] there is an undercurrent of criticism in that Sabinus thinks for himself but badly and confusedly, while Cotta

[1] *B.G.* VII, 62, 2.   [2] *B.C.* III, 51, 4–5.
[3] It has recently been urged in a learned and ingenious book by M. Rambaud, *L'art de la déformation historique dans les Commentaires de César* (Paris, 1953) that Caesar ungenerously depreciates their actions to enhance his own credit but, after a careful re-reading of the relevant parts of the *Commentaries*, I cannot believe that this is so.
[4] *B.G.* VI, 36, 1–2.   [5] *B.G.* V, 28 ff.

56

keeps nearer to the implied purpose of Caesar that his *legati* were to do what they were set to do, that is to hold fast, and 'stay put', as Q. Cicero did. But when his *legati* show initiative, as Publius Crassus in the battle with Ariovistus,[1] or Labienus in the battle against the Nervii,[2] or in 52 in the operations near Paris, he records it in significant words, 'tantis subito difficultatibus ab animi virtute auxilium petendum videbat'.[3] In general, Caesar does not use laudatory phrases about his *legati*. As he does not compliment himself when he wins a victory, so he does not compliment them, but he does show what they achieve, and why, and that is enough.

The purely military appreciation of Caesar's opponents in the *Civil War* is without illusion. The strategic judgement and tactical care and resource of Pompey are not underrated[4] nor the subtlety of Afranius[5] and the vigour of Petreius.[6] They too understood the *ratio belli*, and if they err it is not for lack of military expertness. Their failures are due rather to weaknesses of spirit and intellect on a higher plane: they lacked Caesar's mastery of men and events, his fusing together of wits and will.

Caesar was more than a strategist and tactician; he was a soldiers' general. His legions were the instruments of his purposes, on whom he played with easy mastery and a kind of affection. Nearest

---

[1] *B.G.* I, 52, 7.
[2] *B.G.* II, 26, 4–5.
[3] *B.G.* VII, 59, 6.
[4] E.g. *B.C.* III, 87, 7.
[5] E.g. *B.C.* I, 40, 4.
[6] E.g. *B.C.* I, 75, 2.

to his heart are the centurions, who have the soldierly virtues of the legionaries raised to a higher power. Caesar deplores their loss in reverses and goes out of his way to praise their exploits of courage and steadiness. He is aware that his readers will know that the centurions are the soul of the legions, that it is they who are the agents of the disciplined movements which a Roman general could count upon, without which neither the genius of a commander nor natural courage and *élan* in the troops could achieve victory. Next in the order come the veterans and the veteran legions, who are marked off from the recruits and their formations, which have to work their passage into Caesar's esteem. It was his practice not to dilute his veteran formations with troops of less experience, and the distinction is preserved and at times stressed in his narrative. When at Vesontio he needed to hearten his army to advance against the formidable Ariovistus he says that if others fail him he will march with the Tenth Legion alone,[1] and the rest of his campaigns show that his words were not forgotten.

No one could say of Caesar what Anatole France said of Napoleon: 'il pensait ce que tout grenadier dans son armée pensait', nor suppose that he visited the camp-fires of his troops like the King before Agincourt in *Henry V*. But here and there he records what the soldiers said in jest or earnest, and here and there his *elegantia* stoops to the diction of the

[1] *B.G.* I, 40, 15.

58

camp, the *sermo castrensis*. He inspired in his troops a patience in hardship and a vehement will to victory like his own until, as at Ilerda, they raged at the thought that the enemy might escape them.[1] At Gergovia they pressed on beyond the bounds of his design and were rebuked for it when it led to a reverse.[2] But at Pharsalus when the Pompeians were ordered not to meet their charge half-way so that Caesar's troops might reach the clash out of breath, they halted with instinctive warcraft, and then thrust the attack home. Caesar's criticism of Pompey's order, that troops are weakened by standing fast,[3] implies praise for his own legionaries who had learnt from Caesar to think coolly and still to strike vehemently when the moment came.[4]

Ruthless as Caesar was towards alien enemies, he reveals a provident care for the welfare of his troops. He is patient and resourceful to avoid exposing them to risks. In the campaign in Ilerda he is resolute not to force a battle which will involve his army in heavy losses in the destruction of another Roman army, which he seeks to avoid from generosity as well as policy.[5] Nowhere in the *Commentaries* is there a contumelious word for the Roman troops who fought against him, and everywhere he does the fullest justice to those who fought on his side.

The study of the *Commentaries* comprises the study of Caesar's advance in the arts of a general,

---

[1] *B.C.* I, 64, 2.   [2] *B.G.* VII, 52.   [3] *B.C.* III, 92, 4.
[4] *B.C.* III, 93, I.   [5] *B.C.* I, 72, 3.

little as Caesar was concerned to explain why he began a good general and became a better one. There have been generals—Alexander, Aurelian, Gustavus Adolphus, Marlborough—who saw in cavalry the decisive arm in battle. To Caesar, as to most Roman commanders, cavalry was, to begin with, only a helpmeet to the 'queen of the battle-field', infantry. But it may be seen how he, and his lieutenant Labienus, made an increasing use of it in Gaul, and in the great crisis of his seventh campaign he countered the cavalry of Vercingetorix with horse-men recruited in Germany. When, as in the Ilerda campaign, he had superiority in cavalry he used it to great effect, and in the Balkans, and later in Africa, he found ways of defeating or neutralizing the Galatian or Numidian cavalry of his opponents. In his last battle, at Munda, the turning-point in the battle followed a cavalry movement, though it is not clear that Caesar initiated it himself. But, in general, it looks as if he had no great faith in cavalry unless it was closely backed by infantry, except for reconnaissance, raiding and pursuit.

If Caesar was not in any marked way a cavalry general, still less was he an admiral. He had not Pompey's appreciation of the use that could be made of sea power, but it is instructive to observe how he gives his mind to overcoming the difficulties pre-sented by the sea-going ships of the Veneti and by the need to move and land the legions in Britain. In the Civil War he has not the means to match the fleets of his opponents. His reply is to observe the weather habits of the Adriatic and act so as to make them his allies. On the whole, he left the conduct of the war at sea to others, especially to Decimus Brutus. It is even possible that he doubted if *ratio belli* could play its proper part on an element which most Romans distrusted.

Pompey in his youth had been renowned for his *celeritas* which Cato himself praised even after Pharsalus.[1] Caesar was a master of immobility if he could make time fight for him as in the opening phase of his first campaign against the Belgae, but his instinct was to strike quickly and to strike hard, and when he struck he struck right home. After his defeat at Dyrrhachium, when for a moment 'omnia erant tumultus timoris fugae plena', he describes the reasons why Pompey fell short of completing his victory, the chance which 'celeritate insequentium tardata nostris salutem adtulit'.[2] Even so, Caesar had to disengage his army, to move it out of disaster's way and to restore its morale. His appeal to his troops culminating in the words 'dandum omnibus operam, ut acceptum incommodum virtute sarciretur'[3] echoes the spirit of a soldier's general.

Finally, the reader can observe a growing expertness in judgement of terrain and an advance in skill in the use of field fortification to economize his strength, to protect his manœuvres and to give

[1] *B. Afr.* 22, 2.   [2] *B.C.* III, 70, 2.   [3] *B.C.* III, 73, 5.

himself the possibility of surprise. He was not alone in this, and he clearly appreciates this kind of resourcefulness in his lieutenants, and above all the readiness of his legionaries to fight with the spade as well as the sword. When all is said and all the sides of warfare are taken into account, the reading of the *Commentaries* is deservedly commended by Napoleon to the constant study of anyone who sought to make himself a master of the art of war.

4

STYLE AND PERSONALITY

WHAT has appeared in the preceding three chapters, the plain unadorned matter-of-fact character of a *commentarius*, the content of which is so predominantly a narration of military events militarily viewed by a military man, would make a reader expect to find the style of the *Commentaries* uniform almost to the point of monotony. It would be very much the same story told in very much the same way, for it need not, or should not, be told otherwise. But there is more than this: Caesar had the habit, it would seem, of deciding what was the best word for this and that, and then never admitting any other. As is pointed out in the first chapter (p. 16) Latin had been a rather luxuriant language with several words meaning very much the same thing, but since the second century B.C. it had been pruned. This process was carried further by Caesar, so that when the same thing happens it is natural and proper to find the same words or phrases used about it. The precision of his mind works in with his interest in words and language, tends to reflect the recurrence of an idea or of an action in a repetition of words and phrases, and this helps to produce a uniformity of diction.

Granted that this is so, the intensive study by so

many scholars of Caesar's vocabulary and phraseology has not been in vain. It has shown how little ambiguity or vagueness has slipped past the guard of Caesar's sharp clear mind to cloud the *elegantia* of his style.[1] Apart from faults in the manuscript tradition of the text, there may be passages in which some report or the like by another hand has not been fully converted by Caesar into his own diction. This may be so more often in the *Civil War* than in the *Gallic War*, if, as is probable, Caesar produced parts of the *Bellum Civile* under pressure of haste. But when account is taken of these possibilities, the major part of the *Commentaries* shows the special qualities of the Caesarian style.

The precision in the use of words, the *pura et inlustris brevitas* which Cicero praises in Caesar's writing is a constant phenomenon. But as the *Commentaries* proceed, they exhibit some difference of style. It has often been observed how the First Book of the *Gallic War* is more formal in the *commentarius* manner than the Second, and that after the Second the style becomes slightly more informal in the next four books. The Seventh Book has more movement still and, as it were, flows faster, and the same is true of the books of the *Civil War*. The constructions and run of sentences become freer, and there are changes of a kind which suggest

---

[1] 'Elegantia' imports the choice of the right word, rather than any elaboration or elevation of style. See E. E. Sikes in *Camb. Anc. Hist.* IX, p. 764.

a change of habit rather than a reasoned change of preference in the search for the right word. Such a change of habit is hard to understand if Caesar composed the first seven books of the *Gallic War* in one continuous literary activity within a short space of time. It is in fact a strong, perhaps the most cogent, argument for the view that the *Gallic War* was written in stages over a number of years. If this is so, it may have been quite natural for Caesar to become less concerned to preserve the stylistic effect that belongs to the *commentarius* form. There appears, indeed, in the First Book of the *Gallic War* to be deliberate avoidance of literary polish. Thus in the third chapter two successive sentences begin with the phrase 'ad eas res conficiendas'. In neither sentence can the phrase be merely struck out as an interpolation without harming the sense, and it is hard to suppose that the repetition is due to hasty writing. It appears rather to be a deliberate roughening of the style. So too there are instances in which the antecedent to a relative is repeated in the relative clause, with something of the cumbrousness which is characteristic of Roman formal documents. This kind of thing disappears in the later books of the *Gallic War*. In the first six books we do not find speeches in *oratio recta*. It is necessary to give the gist of what was said on occasion, but this is done in *oratio obliqua*, thus avoiding the dramatic literary effect of a fictitious speech in direct speech which is the ornament appropriate to the literary character of *historia*. In the Seventh Book there is one complete speech in *oratio recta*, that of the Gallic chief Critognatus during the siege of Alesia.[1] Critognatus urges his compatriots to do as they once did when the Cimbri and Teutoni invaded them and feed upon those who are unfit for war. The striking character of this suggestion is used by Caesar to justify the insertion of the speech—'non praetereunda videtur oratio Critognati propter eius singularem et nefariam crudelitatem'. But when one reads the speech one finds that the singular and nefarious cruelty plays a small part in it, and what one remembers is what Caesar may have meant his readers to remember—the difference between the transient raid of the Cimbri and Teutoni and the eternal yoke of iron which Rome and Caesar are placing on the necks of the Gauls.

A somewhat subtler use of the same device is to be found in the speech in the same book,[2] in which Vercingetorix defends himself before his country-men when they accuse him of treachery. The speech is in *oratio obliqua* except that in two places with peculiar dramatic force there is a sudden turn to *oratio recta*. The first is '"Haec ut intellegatis" inquit "a me sincere pronuntiari, audite Romanos milites"', and the second is as dramatic— '"Haec" inquit "a me" Vercingetorix "beneficia habetis, quem proditionis insimulatis; cuius opera sine vestro sanguine tantum exercitum victorem fame

[1] *B.G.* VII, 77, 3–16.　　　　[2] *B.G.* VII, 20.

66

paene consumptum videtis; quem turpiter se ex hac fuga recipientem, nequa civitas suis finibus recipiat, a me provisum est."' A good critic has well observed the skill with which the first 'a me' in this passage is thrown into relief by its position between 'inquit' and 'Vercingetorix',[1] and the same device is used again to underline the self-sacrifice of the centurion Marcus Petronius,[2] or the fatal plea of Sabinus at the council of war that preceded the destruction of his army.[3]

In the *Civil War* there is one speech, or rather a pair of speeches, in *oratio recta*—those of Curio before the disaster which befell him in Africa;[4] and here Caesar violates his general rule to give an impression of the fiery spirit of his friend. Caesar plainly cared much for Curio, and the speeches are an epitaph. They are fictitious in the sense that the phrasing is Caesar's—with the brilliant ending 'Equidem me Caesaris militem dici volui, vos me imperatoris nomine appellavistis. cuius si vos paenitet, vestrum vobis beneficium remitto, mihi meum restituite nomen, ne ad contumeliam honorem dedisse videamini.' And there is another exception in the short speeches of Pompey and of Labienus before the battle of Pharsalus—the fanfare of pride before the cold narrative of the battle itself.[5]

The plainness of the narrative style, combined

[1] H. Oppermann, *Caesar, der Schriftsteller und sein Werk*, p. 82.
[2] *B.G.* VII, 50, 4–6.   [3] *B.G.* V, 30.
[4] *B.C.* II, 31–2.   [5] *B.C.* III, 86–7.

with the brevity in which Latin surpasses other great languages, can produce a singularly striking effect without any use of rhetorical ornament. For example, at the crisis before Alesia when the relieving army is making its final effort from without, and Vercingetorix is making a desperate sortie from within, Caesar chooses a place where he can see what is happening and dispatches help, now here, now there, to his lieutenants; until at last, when almost all seems lost, there comes the simple undramatic sentence—'accelerat Caesar, ut proelio intersit',[1] then the one vivid touch—'eius adventu colore vestitus cognito'. This is not for picturesque effect, it is that the colour shows the *imperator* himself is there in his battle-cloak. The battle reaches its climax, until in a sharp *staccato* come the brief sentences, like blows that hammer defeat into victory:[2] 'Nostri omissis pilis gladiis rem gerunt. repente post tergum equitatus cernitur; cohortes illae adpropinquant. hostes terga vertunt; fugientibus equites occurrunt. fit magna caedes.' There is hardly a word that is not pure prose, but the effect is epic. Whether the effect is deliberate artistry or whether Caesar wrote down or dictated straight after the battle exactly what happened and then saw that it was good, no one can say. What is certain is that it is hard to imagine how better it could be done, and it was done within the economy of the *commentarius*.

[1] *B.G.* VII, 87, 3.　　　[2] *B.G.* VII, 88, 2–3.

The battle pieces of Caesar, indeed, stand by themselves in ancient history-writing if we except the highest efforts of Thucydides in his Seventh Book. The best worth examination is the battle with the Nervii, a desperate encounter battle.[1] How concrete is the picture of the place where the Romans halt, how skilful is the suggestion that Caesar had after all done what a good general could do (despite Napoleon's strictures) in his first disposition, how sudden the attack comes; then the phrases which show what the moment needed—'Caesari omnia uno tempore erant agenda'; then follow three chapters in which the growing confusion of the battle, the quickening of its tempo are reflected in the rhythm and in the grammatical construction of the sentences until the climax is reached when Caesar's Gallic cavalry rides for home bearing the news: 'Romanos pulsos superatosque, castris impedimentisque eorum hostes potitos.' In these chapters there is no word of Caesar. The battle is for the moment out of hand. And then the next chapter begins with the word 'Caesar', and there follows the brilliant little description of his own intervention, how he snatches a shield and rallies his troops. The tide of battle halts and then turns, and the rhythm makes it audible to the ear— first the spondees of the halt and then the movement again—'Cuius adventu spe illata militibus ac redin-

---

[1] *B.G.* II, 18 ff.; this analysis owes much to the insight of Oppermann, *op. cit.*, pp. 56 ff.

tegrato animo' and so on. (It is to be remembered that ancient narrative was written, or dictated, to be read aloud.) And then Caesar again, but this time not the fighting soldier but the disposing commander —'Caesar, cum septimam legionem, quae iuxta constiterat, item urgeri ab hoste vidisset, tribunos militum monuit.' Then the steady advance to victory and with victory the phrases that praise the enemy—how after all they had performed what was almost a military miracle: 'Hard it was what they had done but their high spirit had made it easy.' The battle had been a desperate affair: it is described as no other battle in Roman literature. Pharsalus is another story: there we do not find the concreteness of the setting, still less the part that Caesar himself played in the actual engagement; instead the perfect formal description of a battle as a work of military art—almost a game of military chess, the unconscious hint of the fact that by then Caesar had become a virtuoso in the art of war, almost an impersonal directing intelligence.

Thus it may be seen that Caesar's *Commentaries*, whether of his set purpose or not, reflect the personality of the writer, and his mind. It is to be remembered that Caesar is not content to do no more than set down simply a string of events. By now the Romans had come to expect more than that. Hirtius had praised Caesar's 'verissima scientia suorum consiliorum explicandorum'.[1] Caesar is

---

[1] *B.G.* VIII, *Praef.* 7.

concerned not only with actions but with the springs and motives of actions. There had, in fact, been a reaction against the mere annalistic record of events. Fifty years before Caesar, Sempronius Asellio had written: 'nobis non modo satis esse video, quod factum esset, id pronuntiare, sed etiam, quo con-silio quaque ratione gesta essent, demonstrare.'[1]

While Caesar's style is in general not ornamented with rhetorical devices, the *Commentaries* contain passages in which there is a formal composition which might be due to the desire to produce an artistic effect. For example, it has been observed that in the opening chapter of the first book of the *Civil War* the personages who take part in the debate in the Senate are so enumerated as to pro-duce a definite effect. But this may be due rather to Caesar's orderly mind than to the employment of a rhetorical arrangement for effect. If we may suppose that the stylistic effectiveness of the account of the battles against the Nervii and before Alesia is due not to conscious art but to the vividness of the events in Caesar's mind as he wrote, we may sup-pose that a dramatic quality in Caesar's narrative, where it is found, is the direct unartificial effect of the *vivida vis animi* with which he remembered as well as acted. It is the strong impact of Caesar's mind, rather than conscious art, that creates his style, where it rises to distinctiveness. It may march along, orderly as a legion, setting out intelligibly

[1] H. Peter, *Hist. Rom. Rel*[2]. I, p. 179.

and with intelligence the course of action or the *ratio belli* and practical calculations that are the springs of action. Most of what happens seems to be inevitable, almost remote, without emotion. Thus, when Caesar has described the surprise attack on the Usipetes and Tencteri, he continues: 'at reliqua multitudo puerorum mulierumque— nam cum omnibus suis domo excesserant Rhenumque transierant—passim fugere coepit, ad quos consectandos Caesar equitatum misit'.[1] This is not a device to leave his readers to imagine the scene for themselves; nor is it the conscious hardening of his heart; it is that his heart is not awake. But when, at Dyrrhachium, his own army breaks so that it is out of hand, then 'eodem quo venerant receptu sibi consulebant *omniaque erant tumultus timoris fugae plena*, adeo ut, cum Caesar signa fugientium manu prenderet et consistere iuberet, alii dimissis equis eundem cursum confugerent, alii ex metu etiam signa dimitterent, neque quisquam omnino consisteret'.[2] Here, as Caesar lives again through this crisis in his fortunes, the plain style is for a moment infused with the vividness of his recollection. When the army of Curio is routed in Africa the climax is reached with almost the same phrase: 'plena erant omnia timoris et luctus'.[3] Here Caesar is stirred by the thought of that disaster which broke the victorious course of the war and by his sympathy for his troops, but above all he records the death of his

[1] *B.G.* iv, 14, 5.   [2] *B.C.* iii, 69, 4.   [3] *B.C.* ii, 41, 8.

72

friend in expiation of his fault—'at Curio numquam se amisso exercitu, quem a Caesare ⟨suae⟩ fidei commissum acceperit, in eius conspectum reversurum confirmat atque ita proelians interficitur'.[1]

As in Caesar's account the swift achievement of victory before Alesia once the tide of battle has turned is reflected in a rapid *staccato*, so the urgency of speed in a supreme effort may be reflected by a use of the historic present to a degree rarely found elsewhere in the *Commentaries*. Once Caesar has crossed the Rubicon it is for him all-important to sweep down Italy and above all, if possible, to intercept the retreat of Pompey across the Adriatic. In the chapters which describe this effort there are found at least as many historic presents as in all the rest of his writings put together. This is to be explained not so much by the desire to impress the reader by a kind of rhetorical device as by the subconscious revelation of Caesar's own vehement desire to finish the war at a stroke. The reader would know that Caesar did not in fact achieve this purpose; what mattered was not what the reader would think but what Caesar felt and hoped and strove to attain.

Thus the study of Caesar's style may be revealing for the study of Caesar's mind and will, especially at moments of crisis. When he is describing the doings of his lieutenants the style is, in general, less emphatic, less vigorous, though even in these, as in

[1] *B.C.* II, 42, 4.

the account of Curio's campaign or, again, in that of the disaster to the army of Sabinus and Cotta and the events that led to it, there is a more dramatic treatment of the situation. It becomes more personal as Caesar's imagination of what must have happened is engaged. On the whole, though, the operations of the *legati* are described so that the military quality of their actions, their *consilia*, so far as these are their own and not Caesar's at one remove, can be appraised, but that is all.

None the less, a close study of those parts of Caesar's narrative which rest on the reports of his lieutenants may reveal stylistic touches which are taken over in a kind of submerged quotation. Thus in the account of the siege of Massilia the texture of the narrative appears to show three strands, the matter-of-fact technical siegecraft of Trebonius, a livelier tone in the report of naval operations which would be supplied by the admiral Decimus Brutus, and the occasional comment of Caesar himself.

There is a habit of Caesar which may reflect more than one stylistic motive. When he is describing actions or the springs of action he invariably refers to himself in the third person by his name Caesar. This may in part be due to his adoption of the *Commentarius* form, though that form is found elsewhere to admit the use of the first person by a narrator. It is true that the use of the third person has an air of objectivity, almost of detachment, which may subtly win the reader's assent; though it may seem to be monotonous, it serves the clarity of the narrative: it perhaps needs no other explanation. But it may, at least in part, be a revealing mannerism. Here and there, outside the *Commentaries*, what seems to be good tradition shows Caesar referring to himself by his name, where the first person would seem more natural. The famous words 'You carry Caesar and Caesar's fortune' is hardly an example, for his boatman needed to be told who his passenger was. But the equally famous dictum that Caesar's wife must be above suspicion might have run 'my wife' or 'the wife of a Pontifex Maximus'. To say 'Caesar's wife' has something that is in a way more than either, something that has a sharper impact. The effect may be illustrated, though it is no more than an illustration, by the high-riding words that Shakespeare makes Caesar use in his decision to go to the Senate House on the Ides of March, when the omens give their warning of danger:

> The gods do this in shame of cowardice:
> Caesar should be a beast without a heart
> If he should stay at home to-day—for fear.
> No, Caesar shall not: danger knows full well
> That Caesar is more dangerous than he:
> We are two lions litter'd in one day
> And I the elder and more terrible,
> And Caesar shall go forth.

To return to what is evidence. When at Pharsalus Caesar saw his enemies broken he spoke words that may well have been truly recorded by Asinius Pollio,

75

who stood at his side. 'Hoc voluerunt'—they would have it so; and then—'tantis rebus gestis Gaius Caesar condemnatus essem, nisi ab exercitu auxilium petissem'.[1] Here, in this *cri du cœur*, his name springs to his lips, it adds something, it throws into the scale his belief in his own greatness. It is thus possible that the constant use of his name in the *Commentaries* is not only a convention or a mask of objectiveness, but includes, as it were, the natural, almost automatic, expression of his conscious pre-eminence.

[1] Suetonius, *Divus Iulius*, 30, 4.

5

CERTAIN PROBLEMS

1. THE 'GALLIC WAR'

(a) Time of Composition

THE question when Caesar composed his own *Commentaries* on the Gallic War (*B.G.* I–VII) cannot be settled beyond dispute. Mommsen argued that Caesar must have written both Book I and Book VII at about the same time as each other, for in Book I (28, 5) he says that the Aedui with Caesar's permission gave lands to the Boii and adds that afterwards '(postea) in parem iuris libertatisque condicionem atque ipsi erant receperunt', and in Book VII (9, 6) he says that after the Boii had been defeated in the campaign against the Helvetii he had placed them in Aeduan territory and added them to that community, and in the next chapter he says they were subordinate (*stipendiarii*) to the Aedui. Mommsen deduces from this that they remained subordinate until the year 52 and were granted equal sovereign rights with the Aedui after the collapse of the general rebellion. Thus when Caesar wrote Book I he already knew what was to happen to the Boii in 52. Against this it can be urged that in the same Seventh Book (17, 3) they are mentioned as though they were distinct from the Aedui, and later (75, 2 and 4) the contingent they sent to the relief of Alesia is not listed with the Aedui and their clients, but separately as though they are an independent people. The list in chapter 75 seems to be based on a document which should be good evidence for the status of the Boii. As in chapters 9 and 10 Caesar is concerned to show that in protecting the Boii he was acting as a loyal ally of the Aedui, he may have misrepresented the degree of their independence, which is assumed in chapter 17 and revealed in chapter 75. It is just conceivable that the Aedui granted equality, indeed independence, to the Boii early in 52. But though this is conceivable, it is improbable. It seems on the whole more likely that the Aedui, who in 58 are said to have prized the military value of the Boii, proceeded, quite soon after they had granted them lands, to place them on an equality with themselves as a sovereign community. This would most naturally explain the reference to this action in Book I, for it would then complete the picture of the good treatment of the Boii after the campaign against the Helvetii, whereas, if it happened six years later, it seems to be a quite irrelevant addition to the narrative of what happened in 58. Thus the passages about the Boii would not support the thesis that Book I was written as late as 52 B.C. or soon after, but rather that it was written soon after the events which it describes.

There is a passage (IV, 21, 7) in which Caesar, writing of the events of 55, says of a Gallic chief,

Commius—'quem ipse Atrebatibus superatis regem ibi constituerat, cuius et virtutem et consilium probabat et quem sibi fidelem esse arbitrabatur cuiusque auctoritas in his regionibus magni habebatur'. Three years later Commius deserted the cause of Rome, and Mommsen suggests that the words 'et quem sibi fidelem esse arbitrabatur' reveal Caesar's knowledge that he later ceased to be 'fidelis'. But, acute as this suggestion is, it is not necessary. Caesar's belief that Commius was faithful to the Roman who had placed him so high and thought of him so highly was relevant to his employment by Caesar as envoy to Britain, and mention of it need not imply that Caesar knew how he behaved in the national crisis of 52 B.C. It may be added that if these two passages did show that Book I and Book IV contained something that Caesar did not know until 52 B.C. they would not *prove* more than that these two books were still unpublished, so that Caesar could add something here and there; they would not *prove* that the books were still unwritten when the year 52 began.

There is one other passage which has appeared to some scholars to indicate that Caesar wrote all his commentaries on the Gallic War at one time. Hirtius in the Preface to the *Bellum Gallicum*, Book VIII, says of Caesar's commentaries: 'ceteri enim quam bene atque emendate, nos etiam quam facile atque celeriter eos perfecerit scimus'. Dr Rice Holmes says 'if the statement that the *Commentaries* were

written "easily and rapidly" is not absolutely in-
consistent with the view that each book was written
during the comparative leisure of the winter following the campaign which it describes, the natural
meaning is that the whole work was the result of a
continuous effort'.[1] And a little later[2] he writes:
'Hirtius's words show that he had himself witnessed
the rapidity with which Caesar wrote his *Commentaries*: therefore it is morally certain that they were
written at one time; for the other theory, besides
involving a forced interpretation of the Latin, would
oblige us to assume that Hirtius regularly spent his
winters with Caesar in Cisalpine Gaul.' No student
of Caesar will fail to pay great attention to the
opinions of Dr Rice Holmes, but Hirtius, who is
speaking not of himself alone when he says 'nos'[3]
but also of Balbus, to whom the Preface is addressed,
can very well say that his friend and he had observed
how quickly and easily Caesar wrote his Commentaries if each of them had seen him write one or
more of them—'ex pede Herculem'. Also he may,
for all we know, have been with Caesar in Gaul for
several winters at least.

The field is, in fact, left open for the second
hypothesis, that the *Commentaries* on the Gallic
Wars were written at intervals of time. For that
hypothesis strong arguments can be advanced. Once

---

[1] *Caesar's Conquest of Gaul*[2], pp. 203–4.   [2] *Ibid.* p. 209.
[3] Where he is speaking of himself alone he uses the first person
singular 'contexui', 'susceperim', etc.

Caesar had conceived the idea of writing an account of his campaigns in Gaul it would be the most sensible and convenient thing to do so at the earliest possible moment after each of them. One at least of his motives was to tell the story himself, and if he fell in battle it would serve his purpose to have told the story up to the end of the previous campaign. And there is no good reason to think that Caesar believed himself to bear a charmed life. Moreover, the material he would use would be available at the end of each campaign, and more easily used while the memory of the events was fresh and while his subordinates were at hand for consultation about reports they had recently written. They might not always be at hand. It is theoretically possible that the written reports and war diaries of Caesar's *legati* would provide everything that appears in Caesar's account of their doings and of the motives that guided them, but it is not probable; and if the accounts needed more interpretation by the *legati* than their written reports or war diaries would provide, it would be strange if Caesar did not find it convenient to combine reports and interpretation into one written narrative. In *B.G.* III, 17–27, we have an account of the operations of Sabinus and those of P. Crassus in the year 56, which combines action and interpretation in a way most easily understood if Caesar was able to discuss the operations with these *legati*. Sabinus was killed in 54 B.C.; P. Crassus was sent to Rome in the winter of 56/55, and he is not heard of except as at Rome until he travelled to Syria late in 54, where, in the next year, he met his death. It seems reasonable to suppose that Caesar decided what he meant to say about their operations of 56 B.C. while the two *legati* were still with him, and it is hard to see why he should not have written down at once what he meant to say. The same consideration may apply even more strongly to Caesar's account in *B.G.* v, 26–37 of the disaster of Sabinus's army and the events that led up to it, for which Caesar would have to depend on a few informants who escaped from the battle, and (v, 52, 4) some Gallic prisoners who would know that the Romans in the camp after a sturdy defence killed themselves rather than surrender.

A further reason is to be found in the fact observed by Ebert, that while there are references forward within the account of each year, there are none, except for the two doubtful instances that have been mentioned, between the accounts of different years. This seems improbable if the accounts of the seven years were all written at the conclusion of the whole septennium. Finally, there is a development of style, a movement towards an easier and freer[1] composition, which would be very remarkable if it happened within the space of a few weeks or even months, but quite explicable if the whole period of composition was to be measured in years. It is

[1] See especially J. J. Schlicher, 'The development of Caesar's narrative style', *Class. Phil.* XXXI (1936), pp. 212 ff.

agreed that the style of *B.G.* I is stiffer, more old-fashioned as it were, nearer to the *commentarius* manner, than that of *B.G.* VII (see p. 64). This is more readily understood if the period between their composition was long rather than short. To take an instance in which Caesar appears to have made a change in his phraseology: Professor Löfstedt has observed that in the *Bellum Gallicum* Caesar uses 'infimus' twelve times, 'imus' only twice (III, 19, 1 and IV, 17, 3), each time in the set phrase 'ab imo'. In Book VII he uses 'ab infimo' twice (19, 1; 73, 5) and 'ad infimum' at 73, 5. He suggests the possibility that Caesar made a deliberate change from 'ab imo' to 'ab infimo'.[1] If this is so, it is natural to deduce that there is an interval of time between what may be called Caesar's habit of using 'ab imo' and his habit of using 'ab infimo' instead. In *B.G.* III, 19, 1 we read 'paulatim ab imo acclivis', in VII, 19, 1 we read 'leniter ab infimo acclivis'; this suggests a feeling of the superior suitability of 'infimus'. On the whole, it appears to be at least probable that the composition of the *Bellum Gallicum* proceeds at intervals over a period of years.

(b) *Time of Publication*

It is even harder to decide when Caesar published his commentaries on the Gallic War than when he wrote them. It has seemed obvious that if they were written a year at a time, they were published

[1] *Syntactica*, II, pp. 347 f.

as they were written. But it is not so simple ?s that. Publication year by year would, it is true, preclude revision in the light of subsequent events in the absence of some later republication of the whole work. There are, in fact, statements in the earlier books, such as that the troops of the Nervii were practically exterminated, which are proved false by subsequent events. These statements remain uncorrected, but that does not prove that these earlier books *could* not have been corrected (because they were already published) but only that, for whatever reason, Caesar did not correct them.

It has been argued that he published Commentaries, or perhaps small groups of Commentaries, in order to influence public opinion at Rome so that the Senate would feel bound to crown his exploits and approve his acts by a public thanksgiving, as happened at the end of his second campaign (*B.G.* II, 35, 4), his fourth campaign (*B.G.* IV, 38, 5) and his seventh campaign (*B.G.* VII, 90, 8).[1] But in the conditions of ancient book production the publication of a *commentarius* could not have a rapid widespread effect, and Caesar himself says on the first two occasions that the thanksgiving was decreed 'ex litteris Caesaris', and on the third (with a necessary emendation) 'His ⟨rebus ex Caesaris⟩ litteris cognitis Romae dierum XX supplicatio redditur.' These phrases should mean that the Senate on the

[1] L. Halkin, 'La date de publication de la *Guerre des Gaules* de César', *Mélanges Paul Thomas*, pp. 407–16.

84

consideration of a dispatch from Caesar decreed a thanksgiving. This would happen presumably soon after the end of the campaigning season, and the fact is then duly registered in the *Commentaries*, when it occurred. The fact that the three references occur at the very end of a *Commentary* does not prove that they are added after publication, for they are in their natural place on any supposition. It has been observed that the *Commentaries* tend to begin with what may be called echoes of the closing words of the previous ones, so that a reader would know which *Commentary* followed which. From this observation the deduction has been drawn that if all seven *Commentaries* had been published at once this would not have been necessary, whereas if they were published year by year the first commentary would not be numbered Book One, and so the later *Commentaries* would not be numbered either. But this deduction is not cogent, for if Caesar wished he could, in either event, number his *Commentaries*, and whenever Caesar wrote his *Commentaries* and whenever he published them, it would be entirely natural for him to look at the end of each, and this would tend to affect the phrasing of the beginning of the next one.

The first chapter of the Sixth Book, dealing with 53 B.C., speaks of Pompey's 'friendship'. It may be asked if Caesar would make this reference in this form if in, say, 51, when Pompey's friendship was suspect, he was free to omit it or alter it, and that therefore the Sixth Book had been published before 51. But in Book VII, 6, 1, which could not have been completed before the end of 52 at earliest (and may have been completed later still) Caesar speaks of the 'virtus' of Pompey; and if, as late as that, he does not hesitate to speak well of Pompey, there is no reason to think he would wish to do otherwise about Pompey's actions in 53. Thus what is said in Book VI does not help to settle the question whether publication proceeded in stages or happened all at one time.

It may be urged that if the primary purpose of the *Commentaries* is political, this purpose dictates publication year by year. If the *Commentaries* are the report of the democratic general to the People, should not the report be made year by year? But, in so far as Caesar's purpose is political, may it not serve that purpose even better to publish the *Commentaries* all at one time, when in fact a crisis in Caesar's fortunes is seen to be imminent? Any difference in attitude or style can be accounted for by *composition* in stages (see pp. 64 ff.) and does not require publication in stages. It has been argued above that Caesar might well have written his *Commentaries* year by year, so that if he was killed in battle there should be his own story available up to the end of the previous campaign. But this purpose would not require publication year by year, granted that Caesar had followers who would see to it that his *res gestae* were published. After all, he would not take them with him on his campaigns in one single copy, so that they might perish with him.

Apart from two doubtful instances there are no forward references *between* books although there are *within* books (pp. 77 ff.). But this does not disprove simultaneous publication of all seven books unless we suppose that Caesar would have thought it desirable to insert such references in order to knit the whole work together. But apart from the convention of the *commentarius* form, we can quite well suppose that Caesar was satisfied with his work as it stood.

If the *Commentaries* were published year by year, we might perhaps expect to find some reference to them in Cicero's speeches or letters, and no such reference can be found. When Cicero's brother Quintus had joined Caesar in Gaul, Cicero's letters to him do not refer to any published account by Caesar of operations in Gaul, though they do refer to private letters from Caesar. When he writes to Quintus (*ad Q.F.* III, 8, 2) 'Ubi enim isti sint Nervii et quam longe absint nescio' he had either not read, or had forgotten, what Caesar says of them in Book II as part of the Belgae and what Caesar says in the first chapter of Book I about the part of Gaul in which the Belgae live. But too much should not be made of that: an *argumentum ex silentio* cannot be very strong in view of the caprice of fortune which may govern the survival of references.

Caesar's own account of his achievements in Gaul

ended with the failure of the great insurrection in
52. But though this no doubt settled the issue, there
were to be troublesome operations during the next
two years which were left for Hirtius to describe in
Book VIII. Precisely when Caesar published Book
VII alone or Books I–VII as one work is not recorded.
It may be conjectured that Hirtius prepared a draft
narrative of the Gallic events of 51 and 50 at the
close of each of the two campaigning seasons, for
though the preface to Book VIII was written after the
death of Caesar in 44 B.C. it is hardly possible that
Hirtius would have begun then to collect the
material for an account of what happened in 51 and
50 B.C. He shows knowledge of Caesar's intentions
and of the considerations that weighed with him,
which he would hardly know so surely if he was not
in Caesar's counsels at the time of the events.

Caesar's own *Commentaries* on the Gallic War were
already published when Cicero praised them in his
Brutus in 46 B.C. The repeated operations of the
winter of 52/51 left Caesar rather short of time even
to write his account of the events of 52 and it is
possible that he could not have published that book
until after the summer of 51 B.C. There are indica-
tions that he thought of being a candidate for the
consulship at the elections in the summer of 50 B.C.
It is possible that he decided then that the time had
come to publish the whole narrative from his advent
in Gaul to the defeat of Vercingetorix. He may too
have regarded the tiresome operations of 51 as an

anticlimax. It is therefore reasonably probable that the Books I–VII were published towards the end of 51 or possibly early in 50 B.C. That Caesar in VII, 6 speaks of Pompey's 'virtus' does not preclude publication as late as the beginning of 50 B.C., for Caesar was still far from despairing of an accommodation with Pompey. If the crisis that followed had ended in peace, if Caesar and Pompey had come to terms with each other, and if Caesar had secured his election in 49 B.C., then it is conceivable that Caesar would himself have completed the story which would have ended in a triumph before he entered on his second consulship. But that is only a matter of conjecture. Once the Civil War began it was highly improbable that Caesar would concern himself further with his Gallic wars, but it is not surprising to anyone who reads Hirtius's preface that Hirtius did not seek to publish his account of Caesar's last two years in Gaul until after the Ides of March.

On the whole, it seems more probable than not that, while Caesar wrote his seven commentaries on the War in Gaul in stages, he published them all at once.

2. THE 'CIVIL WAR':
COMPOSITION AND PUBLICATION

It has often been maintained that Caesar fought and won the Civil War, or at least fought and defeated Pompey, before he set himself to write about it. This opinion is held by many scholars who believe that

Caesar wrote to justify his actions to his contemporaries, that the *Commentaries* are propaganda. This may be truer of the *Civil War* than of the *Gallic War*, and it was in Caesar's interest that his side of the matter should be known quickly. If this is so, it might seem strange if he waited until the war was won before forging a weapon which might help him to win it and using the weapon by means of publication.

The fact that the Third Book does not even complete the account of what happened in the year 48 has led some scholars to suppose that Caesar left it unfinished because the Ides of March ended all his activities. But there is no systematic development between Books I and II and Book III such as would argue that their composition is separated by any considerable interval of time. There are two certain references in Book III to facts as first known to Caesar 'confecto bello',[1] but that does not prove that the Book was written after his victory in Africa, still less his victory in Spain at Munda. Caesar used the word 'bellum' of a campaign, and the campaign in question would have ended with Pharsalus or, at least, with Pompey's death. But these references do suggest that Book III was not published until after Caesar's return to Rome in the autumn of 47 B.C. For these facts might well not be known to him till then.

There is a view that Books I and II, which cover the military events of 49—with one or two omissions

[1] III, 57 and 60.

—were written before Caesar crossed the Adriatic at the beginning of 48 B.C. by the current calendar.[1] These books show some signs of incompleteness or lack of revision, and this may be due to haste and the desire to have them ready for publication by then. On the other hand, Caesar was actively engaged in the field for half the year 49, and travelling about for most of the remainder of it. Caesar could write as he travelled: he wrote his *De Analogia* during a journey from north Italy to Gaul and what seems to have been a narrative poem entitled *Iter* during his journey from Rome to Spain in 45 B.C. Furthermore, his account of the siege of Massilia and of Curio's campaign in Africa would need little more than the rewriting of reports from his lieutenants which would be available to him in good time. And Caesar would have formulated for himself, and others, the defence of his decision to cross the Rubicon before he reached Rome in April 49 B.C. But, even for Caesar, it would be quick work, and it can be urged that he believed that his operations in the Balkans against Pompey would settle the matter one way or the other, so that he may not have thought it imperative to have these two books ready for publication before he left Italy. Equally, after Pharsalus, Caesar would not need to hasten the publication of Book III, and the publication of two

---

[1] See especially K. Barwick, 'Caesars *Commentarii* und das Corpus Caesarianum, *Philologus, Suppl.* XXXI, 2 (1938), pp. 165 ff., and 'Caesars *Bellum civile*', *Ber. Verh. sächs. Akad.* (1951), pp. 88 ff.

earlier books might wait for the third. Finally, there is no clear evidence in Cicero's correspondence or elsewhere that the *Commentaries* on the Civil War were published about this time. So there is too great an element of doubt to permit a confident assertion that Books I and II were in fact *published* in 48 B.C.

What matters, however, for the appreciation of these three Commentaries is not so much when they were published as when they were written. And it may be enough to suppose that Caesar wrote them as soon after each series of events as he could manage, and went on doing so until, with victory over Pompey secured, and with many other things to do, he ceased to wish to continue the story and published them just as they were. But their character and emphasis do suggest that they were written fairly close to the events they describe, and in the mood of dangerous conflict rather than in the mood of victorious retrospect. There is, indeed, evidence that points in that direction. In the First Book of the *Civil War* Caesar can be detected in a number of inaccuracies, partly by the close examination of the narrative, partly by the comparison of it with Cicero's letters or rival traditions. It is difficult to acquit him of conscious misrepresentation of the facts. He was concerned in the early months of 49 B.C. to spread his own view of the situation and to justify himself, for he sent letters to towns in Italy to give his version. There was some immediate advantage in this, as it would weaken recruitment for his enemies and assist recruitment for himself, and might hinder any movement against him while he was in Spain, and then, later, when at the beginning of 48 he crossed the Adriatic. We cannot trace any such degree of misrepresentation in the *Bellum Gallicum*, though we might trace rather more than we do if we had a good independent tradition to compare with Caesar's narrative. On the whole Caesar had no comparable need to misrepresent what happened in Gaul. Between his occupation of Rome in 49 and the battle of Pharsalus those who could detect most of his misrepresentations were, almost all of them, out of Italy. After Pharsalus he had not any practical present need to misrepresent the truth, nor as good a chance of his misrepresentations passing unchallenged.

Asinius Pollio's stricture cited by Suetonius,[1] though phrased generally, might have had a particular reference to what Caesar wrote in *Bellum Civile* I, for Pollio may have been thinking of the difference between his own account of the opening phase of the Civil War and that of Caesar. To the question *cui bono*? the answer may be given: to Caesar *before* he had won and not to Caesar *after* he had won. If this is the right answer, then perhaps one should deduce that Books I and II were *written*

---

[1] *Divus Iulius*, 56, 4: 'Pollio Asinius parum diligenter parumque integra veritate compositos putat, cum Caesar pleraque et quae per alios erant gesta temere crediderit et quae per se, vel consulto vel etiam memoria lapsus perperam ediderit; existimatque rescripturum et correcturum fuisse.'

by Caesar before he won, and perhaps *published* by him before he had won because, after he had won, the effect of publication would be of less value to him and of less efficacy.

It is at least arguable that Caesar's chief concern was to present to posterity his own version of his case, to relate his *res gestae* as he saw them, rather than to secure some immediate short-range advantage. This may be true of his account of his wars in Gaul, granted that, for whatever reason, he stopped after Alesia. But if this was so, then the operations after November 48 B.C., when the *Bellum Civile* ends, were also parts of his *res gestae*, and it becomes more difficult to see why he did not similarly set out his account of them for the same purpose.

In Book III of the *Bellum Civile* he is concerned to give his own story of his struggle with Pompey and to prove, or at least, to assert, that he had been anxious to avoid a struggle *à outrance*. But when he stops where he does, it may be because he had come to realize that he had nothing more that he need justify, except possibly that he was in Egypt when he was needed elsewhere. And it may be said in defence of Caesar that, when at times he misrepresented events, his account was, in all essentials, what he really believed, even if what he believed fell short of the truth. It is quite possible that, though Caesar did not cease to be a man of letters, he had come to care less for self-justification once he had the supreme justification of success. He seems to have become willing to leave to others the narrative of his victories. And the less he came to care for the conventions of the Republic, the less he was anxious to maintain that he had preserved them. And if he waited until after he had won the war against Pompey to describe it, he need not have described it except truthfully. While Pollio says that Caesar would have substituted a more veracious version for what he had written, it may be that he meant to say that Caesar might have substituted truth for falsehood, however little Pollio really supposed that he would trouble to do so.

Finally, the sharpness of Caesar's references to his opponents before Pharsalus may be due, not to any propaganda motive, which had lost its force when Book III was published, whenever this was, for even if Scipio and Labienus were alive, he had little to gain by speaking ill of them—it was rather, one may suppose, that sharp distaste for people who may be able to do you more harm than you can do them. During the first half of 48 B.C. Caesar's fortunes were highly precarious, and his readiness to come to terms with his opponents, provided the terms suited his needs, was not only to spare bloodshed (which may well have been a sincere desire) but from a reasonable doubt whether he could achieve a military victory. However magnanimous Caesar may have been, he could not be unaffected by the stress of a campaign in which his cool judgement would reveal to him that he had to take more risks than he wished, so much so that he exposed himself to a serious reverse. It is reasonable to suppose that Book III was written more or less as the campaign proceeded, or at least, when he was sharply conscious that it had been, what Wellington said Waterloo was, 'the nearest run thing'.

3. THE DIGRESSIONS

There remains one more problem which concerns or may concern the way in which Caesar wrote and published his *Commentaries* on the Gallic War. Apart from the occasional appearance of an inter- polation which can be ascribed to the accidents that befall the transmission of ancient texts, there are passages, especially geographical or ethnological in content, which may or may not be Caesarian in origin, in particular the excursuses on the Suebi (IV, 1–3), on Britain and its people (V, 12–14) and on the Gauls and Germans, together with an account of the great Hercynian Forest (VI, 11–28). These were once generally regarded as un-Caesarian in style and vocabulary, insertions made at a later period and no part of Caesar's own *Commentaries*. But further stylistic and linguistic investigation[1] has established that, when account is taken of the difference of subject-matter and the possible sources from which they may be in part derived, there are not

[1] Especially by F. Beckmann, *Geographie und Ethnographie in Caesars 'Bellum Gallicum'* (Dortmund, 1930).

sufficient grounds to deny them a place in the original work. If they can be Caesarian, then it becomes an interesting question why they appear in the *Commentaries* and why they appear just where they do.

The digression in Book IV about the unneighbourly practices of the Suebi in spreading devastation round their borders helps to explain why the Usipetes and Tencteri are under compulsion to migrate across the Rhine into Gaul. The account of Britain shows that the island contained, besides an area which may be regarded as Gaul beyond the Channel, far-reaching areas of a different character and population which would make the conquest of the whole island an unprofitable military adventure. Poseidonius, the standard writer of the day on the people beyond the European bounds of Roman power, had underrated the size of the island, and inaccurate as the geography of the excursus may be, it does correct the current view on this matter. The digression on the Gauls and Germans in Book VI displays, as it begins by saying, the difference between the culture, institutions and economic conditions between the countries west and east of the Rhine. It becomes plain that Gaul is a country that is worth conquering and can be conquered and that Germany is not. It tacitly justifies the decision to which Caesar came in the end, that the Rhine was the right limit to the expansion of Roman power. Poseidonius had regarded the Gauls and Germans as essentially one ethnological unit, and so far as the culture that bordered on the Rhine was concerned, he was not without some justification. But when the two areas were more widely viewed, the digression in the Sixth Book comes much nearer to the truth in its emphasis on the general divergence between them. The account of the Hercynian Forest and its fauna seems in part to be based upon what was recorded in Eratosthenes and other Greek writers,[1] and where it is fabulous it stresses the remoteness of what is largely a *terra incognita*. To press forward to conquer Germany was to advance beyond the bounds of reasonable imperialism and military promise. These considerations may then help to explain why these digressions are found, even though such digression might seem more in place in a general historical work in the ancient sense of the word than in the more matter-of-fact economy of a *commentarius*.

But if, as appears at least highly probable, Caesar went out of his way to include in his *Commentaries* these geographical and ethnological digressions, he may have had a second consideration in mind, the claim to have passed beyond the bounds of Roman knowledge, to open new avenues to empire (see above, pp. 38 f.). As can be seen from the Ciceronian correspondence, Roman high society had begun to take an interest in what might be found in Britain beyond the Channel. Caesar's reconnaissance in the year 55 kept that interest alive, and he would be well

[1] *B.G.* VI, 24, 2.

aware of it and the hopes of profitable adventure which nourished it. The more southern Britain resembled Gaul, and the closer the bonds between them, the more Roman hopes and Roman policy might be justified. And while Caesar was contemplating his more serious expedition of 54 B.C. he would be concerned to discover more about the island and its inhabitants. The digression that appears in Book V satisfies curiosity and justifies Caesar's enterprise while at the same time it justifies his withdrawal from the island and the advancement of yet more ambitious plans if, as is possible, he had entertained them. Thus these excursuses may fairly be defended as Caesarian by the appropriateness of their content to his purposes, to what he did or decided not to do.

To turn to the related question why these and other briefer digressions appear just where they do, it is noteworthy that the account of Britain does not precede Caesar's reconnaissance in 55, but reflects what he had come to know and evaluate in the next year. Besides that, it breaks the narrative and it can reasonably be suspected of some derangement of its own order, due perhaps to a misplacing of the sheets on which it was written, and a false insertion of the whole in a narrative already written. In chapter 22, 1, there is a reference made to it, which suggests that it is Caesarian, for a later interpolator would hardly have written the words that refer back to it in the form 'quod esse ad mare supra demonstravimus'. The digression on the Suebi fits well into the narrative, and that on the Gauls and Germans is placed after it has been said that the Suebi were expecting the advance of the Roman army far within their borders, and is followed by a statement referring back to the content of the excursus.

The first chapter of Book I supports the famous statement that all Gaul is divided into three parts by indicating the rivers that separate the racial groups, the Belgae, the Aquitani and the Celts whom the Romans call Gauls. It leads on to the effect of the proximity of the Germans which helps to make the Belgae the most warlike of the three groups and does the same for the Helvetii, the people with whom Caesar is about to be most concerned. It is immediately relevant to what follows at the beginning of the next chapter. The second part of the first chapter gives a further definition of the territories of the peoples of Gaul, so that it is a kind of literary map of the whole area, which helps to make clear the operations of the following year, so that it may be written later, but included in the first chapter so as to complete the picture at that point. So far as that assumption is relevant for the composition and publication of the *Commentaries*, it suggests that, while Caesar wrote the books year by year, Book I had not been published when Caesar turns to describe his partial subjugation of Gaul in the Second Book, so that it remains possible for him in 50 to add to the content of the First Book.

6

THE CAESARIAN CORPUS

U NDER the Empire Caesar's *Commentaries*
had no great vogue. When Quintilian writes
of him it is of him as an orator rather than
as a historian. It is true that Quintilian is more
concerned with oratory than with history, but he
could have brought the *Commentaries* in. Cicero's
praise of the *Commentaries* is known to Suetonius
but otherwise it does not find an echo. It may be
suspected that the merit of *pura et inlustris brevitas*
did not suit Imperial taste—the 'brevitas' of
Tacitus could not claim the negative merit of
'pura' or the practical merit of 'inlustris'. The
Commentaries probably owe their preservation not to
their appeal to literary fashion but to the great name
of their author. To this may be due the fortunate
circumstance that the MSS of Caesar came to
include works of which Caesar was the subject
though not the author—the Eighth Book of the
Gallic War, the *Bellum Alexandrinum*, the *Bellum
Africum*, and the *Bellum Hispaniense*. These works
may receive some consideration here, for though
they cannot claim to rank high (or uniformly high)
as literature, they have some significance by way of
comparison and contrast with Caesar's own
Commentaries.

The author of the Eighth Book of the *Gallic War*
is Hirtius, a man who followed Caesar's fortunes,
perhaps from the beginning of the campaign in Gaul.
He is nowhere mentioned as holding an active
command in Caesar's army, and he may have been a
staff officer with especial duties in Caesar's field
secretariat, and perhaps in attendance on him
during the intervals between campaigns. A careful
study of Book VIII shows a knowledge of the mind of
Caesar and no less of the *legati* Fabius and Caninius.
The last two, especially perhaps Caninius, would
have sent dispatches to Caesar reporting their actions and giving reasons for any requests for assis-
tance or the like, and it is just conceivable that these
were preserved in some archives, but there are de-
tails which Hirtius could hardly have discovered from
such an official source but only from discussions
with the two generals or their subordinates. Fabius,
after doing good service in the Ilerda campaign of
49 B.C., does not appear again either in Spain or in
Caesar's army, and it has been reasonably conjectured that he died a comparatively young man after
that campaign. It is very difficult to believe that if
Hirtius waited until Caesar's death to take in hand a
narrative of the events of 51 and 50 he could have
reinforced any official records by means of personal
contacts so long after the events. It is therefore
reasonable to suppose that he built up his narrative
at the time or soon after, and it is not unreasonable
to suppose that he did so because it lay within the

scope of his normal activities to prepare narratives of
events for Caesar at least so far as Caesar's own
immediate operations were concerned. There is
nothing in the Eighth Book which might reflect an
unfavourable view of Labienus, who deserted Caesar
at the outbreak of the Civil War. It is just possible
that Caesar did not give Labienus as much independent responsibility as he had done earlier because
he had come to distrust him, but there is no hint in
the narrative that this was the reason. The preface
to the Eighth Book need not imply any more than
that Hirtius decided to publish what he had written,
and the preface, like other prefaces in antiquity and
modern times, was probably written after this Book
was complete. Indeed, in view of the fact that
Hirtius was ill for a considerable part of the time
between the Ides of March and his entering on a
busy consulship on 1 January 43, and that he died of
wounds in the early spring of that year, it is difficult
to suppose that he could in those few months have
carried out the difficult task of reconstructing the
events of 51 and 50. Thus the Eighth Book has the
character of a Caesarian commentary covering two
years, minus the activity of Caesar as an author.

The *Bellum Alexandrinum* begins where the *Civil
War* of Caesar ends. The MSS give no indication of
the author's name, and in the time of Suetonius the
authorship of the *Bellum Alexandrinum*, of the
Bellum Africum and the *Bellum Hispaniense* was
uncertain. 'Some,' Suetonius says, 'suppose

Oppius, others Hirtius', 'qui etiam Gallici belli novissimum imperfectumque librum suppleverit.'[1] The last two works, for reasons that will be given later, are certainly not by Hirtius. There are some fairly good, though not compelling, reasons for supposing that he wrote or compiled the *Bellum Alexandrinum*. There are turns of phrase, and here and there a sardonic overtone, which are found in the Eighth Book of the *Gallic War*. In the first quarter of the work there are traces of a Caesarian style, and it is possible that here there is Caesarian material which Hirtius, who was not at Alexandria, may have been permitted to draw upon. The book belies its name, for it adds an account of Caesar's campaign in Asia Minor in which Hirtius was possibly present, and affairs in Spain which look like the narrative of someone whose horizon was bounded by the Peninsula. It is a reasonable conjecture that Hirtius had assembled in one book material from several sources to cover the operations that lay between the end of Caesar's *Civil War* as he left it and the campaign that is the subject of the *Bellum Africum*.

The *Bellum Africum*, though it has not the variety, the shifts of scene and lively sense of personalities that lend interest to the *Bellum Alexandrinum*, has a marked character of its own. It is more nearly in the direct *commentarius* style, written with a cool appreciation of the military expertness of both sides,

[1] *Divus Iulius*, 56, 1.

together with a high appreciation of Caesar's qualities. It is plainly the work of an eye-witness and of an officer of high enough rank to know the general motives of Caesar's strategy. Hirtius did not serve in this campaign and, if he had, he would not have written this soldierly professional narrative, with its directness and its limitation, any more than he would have written its successor, the *Bellum Hispaniense*. The style does not resemble that of the work certainly written by Hirtius. If Hirtius, as his Preface to Book VIII of the *Gallic War* indicates, was concerned to see the tale of Caesar's campaigns complete, he may have promoted the composition of the *Bellum Africum*. If it can be supposed that he himself had prepared some kind of factual basis for Caesar's own *Commentaries*, he may have expected to find in this book something he could make into a work of his own. It may, indeed, have been found among his papers after his death, and, with the easy notions of authorship that haunted antiquity, have been thought to be his own, though whoever wrote the work is entitled to claim the credit for having produced a book that has a personality of its own and reflects its author.

The same is true of the *Bellum Hispaniense*. Dr Rice Holmes may have been over-severe in calling it the worst book in the Latin language. There are other strong claimants. The author was ill-chosen if he was to be the plain recorder of Caesar's last campaign to provide source-material for Hirtius. He was a soldier, possibly of the Tenth Legion, who, as Macaulay says, fought better than he wrote. (At least he could not have fought worse.) He shows no understanding of Caesar's purposes or any clear appreciation of the art of war, but badly as he writes, he does, consciously or not, succeed in reflecting the ebb and flow of emotion in an army as it joins battle.[1] This kind of effect is not wholly banished by his ill-timed attempts at fine writing or misplaced literary allusions, or quite lost in the undigested fragments of information which go to form much of his book.

The inclusion of the *Bellum Alexandrinum*, the *Bellum Africum* and the *Bellum Hispaniense* in the corpus of works on Caesar's achievements, however that inclusion came about, secured their survival as well as that of Hirtius's Eighth Book of the *Gallic Wars*. The remaining extant sources of information add little of value, so that students, especially of military history, have much to be thankful for. It is vain to regret the loss of Livy's books on this period, which might have given an account in part based on writings which contained traditions not so dominated by admiration of Caesar. The independent judgement of a good soldier and a better man of letters, Asinius Pollio, would provide more than a foil to Caesar's greatness, and there are signs in the tradition of some authority hostile to Caesar. As it is, the whole Caesarian Corpus, by what it contains, does

[1] *Bell. Hisp.* 29.

provide material for the study of Caesar's generalship in the way which is only approached, though not equalled, by the sources for the campaigns of Alexander the Great.

Furthermore, a close comparison of the styles of Hirtius and the others reveals interesting differences between them in phrasing and interpretation, and even more enhances by contrast the eminent qualities of Caesar's style and the direct impact of his personality. Apart from the Eighth Book of the *Gallic War* and part of the *Bellum Alexandrinum*, the *Bellum Africum* does provide a kind of picture of Caesar as a soldier's general, undaunted, resourceful and a master of his craft, tested by the skill and initiative of Labienus, and by the fact that the first part of the campaign was an uphill struggle against superior forces.

As under the Empire, so throughout most of the Middle Ages the whole Caesarian Corpus appears to have been comparatively neglected. But with the Renaissance it found a vogue which was enhanced by the rise of nationalism especially in France, the scene of the Gallic Wars. The effect of the *Commentaries* was assisted by the popularity of Plutarch, and as in his own day Caesar was notable by carrying Roman arms across the Rhine and the Channel, so he found a place in the history and tradition of Britain and of Germany. In the sixteenth and seventeenth centuries, as the art of war was more systematically studied, the tactics and military organization of the Caesarian armies were regarded as a compendium of military science. Such writers as the Maréchale de Saxe were never weary of citing Caesar as a model, and finally Napoleon I proclaimed that the study of Caesar's campaigns was a prime requisite for the self-education of a general. In the nineteenth century Caesar appeared to Mommsen the genius who served the cause of democracy, and to Napoleon III the forerunner of the military greatness of France and the new Caesarism. And all this was possible only because of the works of Caesar and of the soldiers who served under him and wrote about him.

GENERAL INDEX

Romans are indexed under the best-known element of their names.

INDEX OF PASSAGES

INDEX OF PASSAGES

INDEX OF PASSAGES